the series on school reform

Patricia A. Wasley
University
of Washington

Ann Lieberman
Carnegie Foundation for the
Advancement of Teaching

Joseph P. McDonald
New York
University

SERIES EDITORS

(Continued)

the series on school reform, *continued*

Teacher Practice Online

SHARING WISDOM, OPENING DOORS

Désirée H. Pointer Mace

Foreword by Ann Lieberman

Teachers College, Columbia University
New York and London

Published by Teachers College Press, 1234 Amsterdam Avenue, New York, NY 10027

Library of Congress Cataloging-in-Publication Data

Pointer Mace, Désirée H.
  Teacher practice online : sharing wisdom, opening doors / Désirée H. Pointer Mace ; foreword by Ann Lieberman.
      p.   cm. — (The series on school reform)
  Includes bibliographical references and index.
  ISBN 978-0-8077-4968-5 (pbk : alk. paper) — ISBN 978-0-8077-4969-2 (cloth : alk. paper)
  1. Teachers—In-service training—United States. 2. Teachers—Computer networks—United States. 3. Teachers—Professional relationships—United States. 4. Media programs (Education)—United States. I. Title.

  LB1731.P545 2009
  371.12—dc22

                                                                        2008055520

ISBN 978-0-8077-4968-5 (paper)
ISBN 978-0-8077-4969-2 (cloth)

Printed on acid-free paper
Manufactured in the United States of America

16   15   14   13   12   11   10   09   8   7   6   5   4   3   2   1

This book is dedicated to my family—Michael, Simone, and Myles—and to Ann Lieberman, mentor, colleague, and friend. I could not have written this book without you.

Contents

Foreword

Fifty years ago I faced a group of 46 sixth graders in a new community adjoining Los Angeles, as a 1st-year teacher. This was before special education or any of the new understandings that we have learned in this half century about students and teachers. I struggled mightily, but learned so much. I yearned to tell people about what I was learning, but there was no time or interest in what teachers were doing in their classrooms.

The world has changed radically, and today we are thankfully interested in what professionals learn, do, and think as they work with students, clients, and patients (Cochran-Smith & Lytle, 1993; Gawande, 2002; Lave, 1996; Schon, 1983). They are all teaching us that there is knowledge created as doctors, teachers, nurses, and other professionals actually do their work. And it is a different kind of knowledge from that of researchers or policymakers. It is the knowledge of practice. This knowledge has long been missing from the discussion about teaching and learning. And it is this body of knowledge that Pointer Mace makes evident in this book.

Because the book reveals her understanding of both teaching and technology, it is a rare find. Both subjects are hugely problematic in making teaching public. How do you show a piece of teaching (without creating a 2-hour film)? What do you select for viewing? How do you make the complexity of teaching simple and accessible without oversimplifying it? These are the very questions that Pointer Mace tackles through her important investigation and creation of several different examples of showing teaching to an audience now slowly becoming schooled in using media to represent teaching practice.

We not only learn from Pointer Mace's examples, but also get *inside* what we need to know to learn the power and possibilities of making our own websites, to learn from our own practice, and to secure a position in the conversation about learning from one's own teaching.

In a real sense, we begin to build a body of knowledge about teaching that fills the tremendous void that many have felt for years. It has long been known that there is so much learning going on all the time in one's classroom, yet until now, there has been no way to codify it, or share it with others, much less *show it*. This landmark book makes possible the joining together of a sensitive knowledge of teaching with an important and deep understanding of how technology can be used as a tool for unveiling the complexities of teaching. Knowledge about both is necessary to finally show teaching in all its complexities—in different contexts with teachers who have different styles, different commitments, and different amounts of experience. Few people have been able to put teaching and technology together in the multimedia representations of practice that form the basis of this book. And fewer have been able to show teaching in such an accessible way. Read this finely written book under the authorship of an exciting teacher and teacher educator, one who has forged a new way of seeing, feeling, and understanding teaching as it is practiced in live, authentic classrooms.

—Ann Lieberman
Senior Scholar, Carnegie Foundation for the Advancement of Teaching

REFERENCES

Cochran-Smith, M., & Lytle, S. (1993). Teacher research: A way of knowing. In M. Cochran-Smith & S. Lytle (Eds.), *Inside/Outside: Teacher research and knowledge*. New York: Teachers College Press.

Gawande, A. (2002). *Complications: A surgeon's notes on an imperfect science*. New York: Henry Holt.

Lave, J. (1996). Teaching, as learning, in practice. *Mind, Culture & Activity*, 3(3), 149–64.

Schon, D. (1983). *The reflective practitioner: How professionals think in action*. New York: Basic Books.

Acknowledgments

I HOPE that I have done justice to the many collaborators with whom I have worked over the past decade to make teaching public. I am eternally grateful to those who opened their doors to let education audiences learn from their practices, as well as to those with whom I worked closely to create multimedia representations of these practices. All the K–12, higher education, and teacher education CASTL scholars; the fellows of the Goldman-Carnegie and Noyce-Carnegie Quest programs; and my students and colleagues over the years have made extensive contributions to my thinking about making practice public.

Overview: Learning from (and with) Technology

I N 1975, in a leafy neighborhood of Ann Arbor, Michigan, my younger siblings and I would spend entire afternoons "playing computer." We got this idea from my mother, who had received her MBA with an emphasis in computer science in the mid-1960s; the legacy of her graduate work included several boxes around our house filled with 3" × 7" manila cards with tiny rectangles cut into them in indecipherable patterns. I would sit inside our big armoire, of dark brown wood with double doors that closed in the middle, and my brother John would write math problems on a punch card and slip it through the doors. Inside, in the dark, I'd wait with a flashlight at the ready and a calculator, and I'd answer the problem (at "lightning speed") and slip it back through the doors, accompanied with extremely loud beeping noises befitting my technical labors. All in all, it took about a minute for our enormous "computer" to answer double-digit multiplication problems, not that much slower than the "personal" computers available at that time—our much beloved (and desk-sized) PET computer was still 2 years off.

Fast-forward to the early 1990s in urban Oakland, California, where I was teaching elementary Spanish bilingual early primary grades. The computer in my classroom was an ungainly Apple IIe with a floppy disk drive that ran exactly three programs: one for 2nd-grade mathematics computation, one for spelling, and one for word processing. When it was working, which wasn't often, my 30 students and I were able to use it to share our written stories, sometimes amazing ourselves with our astonishing use of clip art. The loud buzzing of the dot-matrix printer would often cause my students to plug their ears during our literacy time. But manipulating the machine to deeply reflect the vibrancy of life in our classroom was beyond our capacity at the time.

Today, my computer is about 12 inches wide and an inch thick. It's relatively silent and can process video, record a podcast, check e-mail, and record these words I'm writing—all at the same time. The work I describe in this book would be impossible if my main working tool were big enough for a 5-year-old girl with tortoiseshell glasses and a flashlight to hide inside. My current work owes a tremendous debt to the advances in computer technology over the past 30 years, shifting the power of computing into the hands of nonexperts and making it possible to unveil some of the rich complexities of children's learning.

That's one of the things that this work of "going public" is about—getting a sense of what student learning, and teacher learning, looks like in everyday classrooms. In this book, I'm going to take you into several classrooms. I'm going to talk to you about who those students and teachers are; how I worked with each of them to develop a multimedia online record of their teaching practice; how their practice can be used for teacher learning; and how, by working collaboratively, we began to open classroom doors for public learning.

TRACING THE WISDOM OF PRACTICE

Lee Shulman, the president of the Carnegie Foundation for the Advancement of Teaching, won the 2006 University of Louisville's Grawemeyer Award for his anthology *The Wisdom of Practice* (2004). In it, he talks about how difficult it is to learn from professional teaching experiences because so much of what happens in classrooms instantly "evaporates." I like Lee's title a great deal, because it honors what goes on in classrooms—how teaching is as much something you become as something you learn how to do. But it can be difficult to see how this wisdom travels. My work over the past several years has focused around the questions, How can we make the wisdom of classroom practitioners visible? What happens when teachers go public with their practice, for them as individuals, and for their teaching settings? How does that work get used in different settings for research, for learning in practice, and for the preparation of novices?

LEARNING TO DO COLLABORATIVE DOCUMENTATION OF TEACHING: "TERRY LOOMIS"

The starting point for all these questions is to work to make the teaching practices of individual K–12 faculty members public. In my doctoral dissertation (Pointer, 2001), I was inspired by Ricki Goldman-Segall's (1996) innovative work in digital ethnography to incorporate videos and images of student work into the body of the manuscript. Through pure serendipity, I met Ricki herself the day after learning of her book, and she generously invited me up to Vancouver to learn from her team how they were approaching the task of documenting teaching and learning through digital video. I learned a great deal from Ricki and her colleague Maggie Beers, from how to hold the camera (at my side, monitor facing up, to avoid pointing a camera directly in someone's face) to what kinds of artifacts to collect. Most important, I committed myself to the idea that using diverse media to document teaching and learning allows educators to paint a completely different picture of what classroom practice looks like.

Around this time, California had just enacted Proposition 227—the "English for the Children" initiative on the 1998 state ballot—effectively eliminating many approaches to bilingual children's learning that were strongly supported by research. This was disheartening, to say the least, but I resolved that I would attempt to describe how, even in the wake of this politically motivated initiative, some monolingual teachers were finding creative ways to respond to the linguistic diversity in their classrooms. The classroom I chose for my ethnographic "portraiture" (Lawrence-Lightfoot & Hoffman Davis, 1997) was a very multilingual third/fourth-grade combination classroom in an urban district in Northern California. The teacher, "Terry Loomis" (referred pseudonymously, at her request), worked continuously to develop a responsive and respectful approach to her students' education. The students themselves—native speakers of English, Spanish, Khmer, and Vietnamese—were very aware of the language landscape of their classroom and the power that having command of more than one language might afford them.

As my work progressed, I invited the teacher and students to collaborate with me in the documentation of their classroom—they interviewed each other on video, audiotaped conversations with their families about bilingualism, and illustrated maps of their home and school language use. Interestingly, at the end of the data-collection process, a group of the students surprised the teacher and me by proposing their own multimedia cultural inquiry project, which they completed with my assistance and presented to the rest of the students. It was a fascinating immersion in the challenges and possibilities that taking multimedia tools into the classroom might provide. This work strongly shaped my subsequent efforts through the Carnegie Foundation to make such documentations of classroom practice more widely available to education audiences.

CAPTURING THE COMPLEX PRACTICE OF VETERAN TEACHERS:
YVONNE DIVANS HUTCHINSON

I began that process by working closely with a teacher who has inspired countless students and colleagues over her 40-year career: Yvonne Divans Hutchinson. Her name may be familiar to those of you who have read Mike Rose's book *Possible Lives* (1995), because his first chapter is devoted to her classroom. Yvonne is a mover and shaker in the Los Angeles Unified School District (LAUSD). She teaches in South Central, where she has taught in various schools for the past 40 years. It is electrifying to be in her presence; she is a visionary who has made a commitment to stay in the classroom despite many pressures on her to leave it. A nearby California State University campus wants her to come teach in their teacher education department. She works every summer in the National Writing Project, running workshops as a teacher consultant. LAUSD asks her to make the rounds of their high schools to lead professional development workshops for other English teachers. But the place where she's happiest is her classroom with her 9th- to 12th-grade students, having vibrant debates about society, racism, and gender—all anchored to rigorous literary texts.

The pupils at Yvonne's school, King/Drew Medical Magnet School, are almost entirely African American and Latino. In serving her students, Yvonne asks herself, How can I get my students into rigorous, academic discussions of literary texts? When I met Yvonne, she was focused on starting from her students' strengths in oral language and developing their capacity to engage in academic discussions of literary texts. As happens with many great teachers, her reputation preceded her, and my colleagues and I at the Carnegie Foundation had heard about her classroom discussions. We thought others might agree with our positive assessment of Yvonne, and in fact she shared with us that she'd been asked many times for videotapes of her National Board Certification Portfolio, but she did not have the rights to distribute those videotapes (and didn't want to start a second career as a video bootlegger of her own work!). Like many teachers with successful teaching strategies, however, Yvonne said that she used the strategies for literary discourse on a nearly daily basis, so if I were to come down to Los Angeles for a day, we could document a morning of instruction, view some student work samples, and go from there. Over the coming months, I worked with Yvonne via phone and e-mail to unpack this morning of practice for different kinds of audiences who might want to see her teach.

The resulting website (Hutchinson, 2003) is what my Carnegie colleague Tom Hatch and I called a "Class Anatomy," because we were trying to get audiences quickly into a 2-hour block of instructional time. The multimedia representation of Yvonne's classroom is framed around six brief clips that allow people to see highlights of those 2 hours. Audiences can also choose to watch the entire unedited 2-hour instructional block, as well as an entire 1-hour interview with Yvonne about her practice. In addition, audiences of Yvonne's work can "mine" various other materials from her classroom: her own writings on her practice, professional development materials she has authored, handouts given to the students, examples of student work, and selected video samples from the beginning of the school year and subsequent school year to give a sense of how her practice changes over time.

ENACTING SPECIFIC PRACTICES: JENNIFER MYERS

We don't need to wait until someone is as experienced as Yvonne Hutchinson to be able to learn from his or her teaching, though. Jennifer Myers, for example, is at the other end of the teacher-experience continuum. She was just hitting her stride; when we documented her class, she was at the end of her 4th year in the classroom. Jennifer teaches second grade at Barrett Elementary in Morgan Hill, California, just outside San Jose. I met her through one of her former MA professors at San Jose State, who said to me, "Well, you know, if you're talking about getting websites of practice, I take my students to visit Jennifer Myers's class every year. It would be great if they had a website that they could go and then return to again and again." As a recent alumna, Jennifer had returned every year to her professor's classroom to do demonstration lessons, talk about her struggles and successes, and be a "near peer" mentor for other MA students. She had also just completed a yearlong professional development experience funded by the Noyce Foundation, helping teachers develop a workshop approach to reading and writing instruction.

Like Yvonne's website, Jennifer's multimedia representation of teaching shows one morning of workshop-based instruction in her classroom. Both her readers and the writers' workshop have a similar hour-long structure, with a minilesson, individual conferences, small-group teaching, and a whole-group check in. On the day we documented, we also recorded Jennifer's reflections, videotaped some student interviews about their reading and writing, and asked her to make explicit the connections between her instruction and the California grade-level standards for second-grade literacy.

Like many elementary school teachers, Jennifer had a living history of the year all around the walls of her class. We created "interactive" classroom walls, so that audiences might examine all the student work samples and pedagogical supports that surrounded the children as they worked and quickly follow the unfolding of her teaching over time.

INQUIRY AND COMMUNITY: IRMA LYONS

Many teachers view their practice as oriented around a series of evolving questions. Irma Lyons connected these questions to her curriculum development and brought that questioning stance into her classroom. When she came to represent her scholarship of teaching using multimedia, Lyons wanted to reflect her work in Santa Monica's Will Rogers Learning Community Elementary School to represent the interconnections between visionary artists from the Harlem Renaissance. The outcome project of this unit was a daylong "Harlem Renaissance Museum" in which Lyons's students represented their research on individuals from the period by performing monologues, making paintings, and producing research PowerPoints, among many other learning experiences linked to the unit.

The challenge we faced in trying to represent this process and product was that the Museum was held in the auditorium of the school and was open to the entire school population as well as members of the nearby Santa Monica community. Former students, district administrators, neighbors, and school board members attended the event. Lyons and I wanted to represent the multiple perspectives of this diverse audience with whom Lyons's students shared their knowledge. I worked with a colleague of Lyons's to gather as many on-the-spot interviews by these community participants as possible, and the resulting multimedia representation of Lyons's work is an interactive collage of the faces and voices of the school community. The collage shows not only the ethnic, age, and language diversity of the Museum audience, but also the community members' connections to each other. An image of one student who focused on Langston Hughes is juxtaposed with an interview of her father, as well as with one with a former student of Lyons who'd also "been" Hughes 4 years earlier.

By representing Lyons's work in this way we also created a concrete illustration of what a "learning community" might look (and sound) like. The term *learning community* can often be used as a "feel-good" moniker for any group of people in an educational setting. But Lyons, who is now the principal of the school, saw an opportunity to make visible the connections between the work of her students as a community of learners and the same connections between the artists and visionaries of the Harlem Renaissance community.

LOOKING ACROSS PRACTICES:
EVERY CHILD A READER AND WRITER

The final case of documenting particular classrooms shifts perspective a bit and describes how I engaged in collaborative work with a group of teachers who had all taken part in the Noyce Foundation's Every Child a Reader and Writer (ECRW) program. ECRW was a multiyear, multimillion-dollar investment in three counties in the San Francisco Bay Area on the improvement of the teaching of writing. The writing workshop practices in Jennifer Myers's classroom, in fact, were ones she developed as a participant in the ECRW professional development workshops.

Teachers who participate in identical professional development adopt and adapt the practices to their particular contexts. After seeing Myers's work online, the Noyce ECRW leadership was interested to show the connections between professional development in the teaching of writing and the ways in which multiple teachers adapted the ideas in their classroom practices.

We worked with Brenda Wallace, an experienced teacher of writing and a professional developer with ECRW, to document a 2-day in-service training on the teaching of personal narrative writing (one of several "genre studies" around which Noyce structures its literacy development work). Four participating teachers agreed to partner with us to show how they approached personal narrative in their contexts: Cyrus Limon, a kindergarten teacher in a Spanish bilingual dual-immersion school; Becky Pereira and Rachel Rothman, both second-grade teachers in two different schools; and Mark White, a fifth-grade teacher.

Because the practices involved in these four different settings had a parallel structure—the writing workshop introduction, student independent work, teacher-student conferences, whole-group sharing, and writing workshop closure—we were able to develop a website that allowed audiences not only to look at single practitioners in single classrooms, but also to look *across* practices to see how different teachers introduced ideas about personal narrative writing, engaged in conversations with students about their craft as writers, and jointly reflected on the body of work generated. In the website created from their mutual work, http://www.InsideWritingWorkshop.org (Noyce Foundation, 2007a), the teachers provide descriptions of each event of teaching, commentary on the events, and related student work samples. For the first time, our team was able to provide transcripts of each video clip to support audiences' comprehension.

InsideWritingWorkshop.org is an example of another realm of invisible practices—those that countless professional developers use to guide their adult learning experiences for practicing teachers nationwide. Brenda Wallace's commentary and reflection on her beliefs about professional development are enhanced by the illustrative connections she makes between her own teaching and the four teachers' classrooms in which the ideas about personal narrative writing take flight.

ABOUT THIS BOOK

I have organized the chapters of this book around these teachers whom I've briefly introduced here, not because they are entirely exceptional, but because they are illustrative of teachers' diverse approaches to thinking about sharing their teaching. Are they interested in sharing a legacy of work developed over many decades? Workshopping the effectiveness of explicit strategies learned in professional development contexts? Making their questions about their teaching public so that others can push their thinking? Inviting interested observers to spend days or weeks in their classrooms? Or some other goals? All these teachers have taken a first brave step: to open their doors. My role has been to help represent their teaching in a clear and accessible way that honors the complexity of practice, efficiently brings people into their classrooms without oversimplifying, and gives a sense of the unfolding of practice over time. I want to invite *you* into envisioning how you might share your practice with others and further expand our understandings of classroom work. My hope is that this book contributes to a generous view of teaching and of the individuals who have committed themselves to this profession. Let's begin the journey together!

QUESTIONS FOR REFLECTION AND CONVERSATION

- What are some ideas from these teachers' practice that resonate with you?
- What might be involved in representing your teaching practice online? What story might you tell about your own teaching?

Multimedia Representations of Teaching Practice: Allied Approaches to Making Teaching Public

M Y WORK with K–12 collaborators to go public with teaching and learning has been informed by allied efforts around the country and the world. My teacher collaborators have not been the only practitioners to open their classroom doors to cameras and scanners, or the first to reflect on their teaching questions and their ramifications in daily teaching life. This chapter describes how other projects have worked to address this challenge in various ways and how these strands of scholarship, innovation, and invention intertwine to inform our efforts to create multimedia representations of teaching and learning.

WHAT IS A MULTIMEDIA REPRESENTATION OF TEACHING?

The first question I am inevitably asked when describing my work is, How do you define a multimedia representation of teaching? It's a fair question, and one with multiple answers. I believe that consensus is developing around what an online multimedia record of practice should contain, an anticipation of potential audiences, and evolving literacies of representation: What's in a multimedia representation of teaching (MRT), whom is it for, and how is it read?

My own experience as a K–12 teacher tells me that teaching is multilayered. Even on my smoothest days, when all of Schwab's (1973) commonplaces of teaching effortlessly interknit, I was engaging in multiple tasks simultaneously: thinking about introducing the idea of revision in writing workshop, anticipating that Johanna would finish her work early, tracking anecdotal observations about Brenda's decoding of unfamiliar words, managing my relationship with my veteran colleague in the adjacent classroom, planning for the Bilingual Education Committee's after-school meeting, thinking about a recent shooting in the community, wishing the ice cream truck driving by had a quieter sound system, and so on.

If you came to see me in Room 2, you would need to know something about most of these to understand what you were seeing, with the possible exception of the ice cream truck. But let me tell you, the best-laid lesson plans can be undone by the inopportune arrival of a slightly off-tune rendition of "The Entertainer."

- You'd need to know something about *me*: how did I understand my relationships with children who lived in a community very different from the one I'd grown up in? What aspects of my teaching practice was I working to develop? What were some principal influences on my daily and long-term decision making? What dispositions did I bring to my professional practice? What professional development experiences did I find valuable and of particular relevance to my teaching? What was my reflective response to my teaching and my students' learning that day? What was it like for me to teach in my non-native language?
- You'd need to know something about my *curriculum*: What was I teaching that day? Was it a Spanish-instruction day or an English-instruction day? How did my lesson(s) connect to longer-term planning in that subject area as well as across the curriculum? What influenced the decision about what I was teaching that day (my grade-level planning team? A district-level pacing guide? Federal testing pressures?)
- You'd need to know something about my *students*: How old were they? What languages did they speak at home? How did they respond differently to my curriculum and pedagogy? How did their families' immigration status influence their view of school? How were the learning needs of first- and second-grade students addressed?
- You'd need to know something about my *context and community*: Who were my colleagues and collaborators? What kind of resources were available to us? How many students attended our school? What kind of challenges was the larger community and school district facing at the time?

In my work with K–12 teaching colleagues we have tried to anticipate these questions and others that interested educational audiences would have about our teaching practices.

What Is in an MRT?

An MRT should answer these questions through the careful selection, organization and representation of artifacts of teaching practice. In our case, this meant that, at a minimum, an MRT would include

- Introductory text: Teacher name, school, grade level, and a brief description of what the website represents.
- A video of teaching practice
- A description of how the documentation piece connects to the whole
- Examples of student work
- Descriptions of the school context
- Practitioner reflections

However, different projects have approached the documentation, organization, and representation of these categories of artifacts in different ways.

Whose Teaching Is Shared?

K–12 practitioners. Many MRTs have been created from K–12 teaching practice. As described in Chapter 1, the Carnegie Academy of the Scholarship of Teaching and Learning (CASTL) involved several dozen experienced K–12 teachers, many of whom elected to develop and represent multimedia Scholarship of Teaching projects (Hatch et al., 2005). Some chose to represent selected days of instruction (Aguilar, 2004; Cone, 2003; Hurley, 2001; Lyons, 2001). Others' projects focused on teaching change over time (Lyne, 2001; Pfitzner, 2003; Pincus, 2001, 2005). All were framed around particular questions about or challenges involving teaching practice. Heidi Lyne, for example, created a 30-minute video about her teaching at the Mission Hill School in Boston, asking, "How do students' performances in portfolio assessment reflect their internalization of a school's 'habits of mind'?" Lyne juxtaposed her documentary video with examples of student work from their portfolios, school documents informing the portfolio assessment process, and her own reflective narratives about the challenges experienced by the first cohort of Mission Hill's students to develop and formally present their portfolios.

Magdalene Lampert and Deborah Ball also devoted themselves to recording and sharing K–12 teaching practice; their 1998 volume describes their efforts to document an entire year of their elementary mathematics teaching. With extensive support from their research team, Lampert and Ball (1998) assumed responsibility for teaching mathematics at a local elementary school. They collected every piece of student work, seating charts, reflective journals, chalkboard images, and lesson plans and represented them all in a six-disk HyperStudio "stack." Their work is impressive in scale, but the images of practice have never been put online.

Fred Erickson (1982, 2008) has been documenting classroom life for decades. His work "studying side by side" (Erickson, 2006) with his collaborators at the UCLA Laboratory School involves a view of classrooms as an ecosystem, a "system of simultaneous and continuous multiple influences—with change in one aspect of the system requiring in change in other aspects" (2008). Erickson's interpretive frames for viewing classroom life emerge from the environments themselves. His Classroom Ecosystem Explorer (CEE), still in development as of this writing, promises to invite teaching audiences to explore science teaching and learning along the dimensions of this ecosystem framing.

Some models for going public with K–12 teaching, such as LessonLab .com (LessonLab, 2008) and Teachscape.com (Teachscape, 2008), are intended for purchase by districts or school organizations. Both of these are online tools and frameworks for professional development by practicing teachers. Customers of Teachscape and LessonLab engage in analysis of video of "exemplary" teachers, related student work, and commentary by the practitioner and compare the online lessons with their own teaching practices (Capper, 2002). Teachscape provides "classroom walkthroughs" in which school faculty use wireless handheld technologies to gather teaching and learning data and transmit it to a central location for group analysis. The teaching cases on both sites include introductions to the teachers, descriptions of the content, examples of student work, and alignment with state standards.

Higher education practitioners. Going public with teaching and learning is not only for K–12 teachers. Initiatives like MERLOT.org (MERLOT, 2008) invite higher education professors to share and comment on teaching and learning materials in a peer review environment. The Public Knowledge Project (2008) offers "open journal" and "open conference" systems, building on accepted genres for knowledge exchange in higher education. Other initiatives, such as the Carnegie Academy for the Scholarship of Teaching and Learning in Higher Education (CASTL–Higher Ed), resulted in fellows' posting "snapshots" of their scholarly investigations using the KEEP tool, shown at http://www.cfkeep.org (Carnegie Foundation, 2008a). The "Teaching and Learning Commons," located at http://commons.carnegiefoundation .org/ (Carnegie Foundation, 2008b), builds on a vision of higher education teaching practice with the Scholarship of Teaching and Learning at its center (Huber & Hutchings, 2005). Only a few projects have proposed to examine the entire span of K–20 learning; among them is the Digital California Project from the Corporation for Education Network Initiatives in California (CENIC) (2001; Dolgonas, 2008), which is developing a "high-bandwidth, high-capacity Internet network specially designed to meet the unique requirements of these communities, and to which the vast majority of the state's K–20 educational institutions are connected" (CENIC, 2001).

How Are MRTs Built?

These various projects have used an array of approaches to construct and support multimedia records of practice. Most of the early CASTL websites were built with the Dreamweaver software, an HTML editing program. Similarly, the University of Wisconsin–Madison is one of many teacher preparation programs in which students create their own HTML-based professional portfolios using templates created by the program.

Other initiatives have used online-based tools to make multimedia representations of teaching public. Later CASTL cohorts created their MRTs using the Carnegie Foundation Knowledge, Exhibition, Exchange and Presentation (KEEP) toolkit (Carnegie Foundation, 2008a), a free, open source PHP-based system in which users can upload text, images, and video to individual pages, group them in "galleries," and make them public in the Teaching Commons (Carnegie Foundation, 2008b). As of this writing, more than 50,000 separate pages have been created using the KEEP toolkit. As described above, LessonLab.com and Teachscape.com offer their own proprietary architecture for making teaching public.

Where Are MRTs Located? How Are They Linked to Other MRTs?

Initially, extensive use of multimedia meant that an MRT couldn't be online; Lampert and Ball's groundbreaking 1998 work is presented in a six-CD set. With the ascendance of broadband, projects have been able to host and stream large data files online. Websites like TeacherTube (TeacherTube, 2008) appropriate the look and feel of YouTube.com but are oriented toward K–12 practitioners looking for interesting resources for their lessons. InsideTeaching.org (Carnegie Foundation, 2007) is a "living archive" of teaching practice juxtaposing MRTs alongside perspectives on their uses in teacher preparation and links to the KEEP tools to invite audiences to create and contribute their own MRTs to the collection. I am very interested in the emergence and increasing popularity of Second Life (Linden Research, 2008), a burgeoning virtual world in which entire schools and professional development experiences for teachers "exist" online.

HOW CAN AN MRT BE FRAMED/REPRESENTED?

All these varied approaches to making teaching public face a similar challenge: inventing conventions for their representation that feel intuitively comprehensible and navigable to their audiences. As Steve Krug's landmark book in web design, *Don't Make Me Think!* (2000) exhorts, people don't go to a supermarket and wander around trying to find the milk. They know that it's in the back. But online design is still inventing the conventions for organizing a site visitor's experience of a website. This is hard enough with online equivalents of real-world phenomena, such as shopping. But representing multilayered teaching events, over time, is largely new. Individuals and initiatives invested in making teaching public have to invent transparent "frames" in which to organize and represent their content.

This framing can bridge the realms of traditional and "new media" texts. Ricki Goldman-Segall's pioneering book, *Points of Viewing Children's Thinking: A Digital Ethnographer's Journey* (1996), is a hybrid text: hardbound and multimedia. It is a visionary extension of Kristeva's (1980) conception of *intertextuality*. Goldman-Segall's book shares original research, describing the ways in which young children use various technologies in and out of their classroom. It also engages the audience in a conversation about the text, by leading readers from the paper text to the accompanying website, http://www.pointsofviewing.com (MERLin, 1998), where video excerpts of her data can be viewed. Years ahead of the blog revolution, with its vibrantly connected communities of commenters around a central text, Goldman-Segall invited her readers to respond to the videos and to her analysis, extending the boundaries of her book and the unidirectional flow of knowledge from author to audience. But making visible these "points of viewing" is also a charge and opportunity for developers of MRTs that exist entirely online.

Framed Around a Lesson or Specific Teaching Problem

Some MRTs are framed around a lesson or specific teaching problem. The Teaching and Learning Interchange, at http://www.teachinginterchange .org (Redmond, 2004), contains a series of MRTs around specific science and mathematics teaching methods. Several of the CASTL K–12 fellows (e.g., Boerst, 2003; Cone, 2003; Lyons, 2001; Myers, 2006) developed and shared their scholarship of teaching MRTs around specific lessons or days of instruction, as well as the website on Nancy Beal's (2004) early elementary art classroom. Knowledge Networks on the Web (KNOW), at http:// know.umich.edu/ (University of Michigan, 2008), provides access to classroom video, curriculum materials, and discussion forums around particular teaching problems for middle school science, though many aspects of the site are password protected in keeping with the university's Institutional Review Board (IRB) agreement.

Framed Around an Individual Practitioner or Classroom

Other MRTs are intended to grant access to the classrooms of particular teachers. They may include individual lessons, but expand beyond that to give a sense of the practitioner, her or his students, and their work over time. Many of the websites on InsideTeaching.org (Carnegie Foundation, 2007), particularly those of Marsha Pincus (2001, 2005), Emily Wolk (2002), Anne Pfitzner (2003), and Ellen Franz (2006), are framed in this way. Several sites developed by Tom Hatch and his colleagues at the National Center for Restructuring Education, Schools, and Teaching (NCREST) (2008) also show teaching practice over multiple lessons, such as the fifth-grade unit on life in Colonial New York developed by Martha Andrews (2005). The Digital Edge Learning Interchange (National Board for Professional Teaching Standards [NBPTS], 2008a) offers several "exhibits" from 64 different classrooms of National Board–certified teachers in various grade levels and subject areas. Countless K–12 practitioners have created websites for their classrooms intended to display student work and communicate classroom news with parents and caregivers; these websites can be housed on school or district servers (Gray, 2008; Renz, 2008) or even on teachers' own proprietary domains (Campioni, 2007; Packer, 2008). Increasing numbers of teachers have blogs (e.g., Davis, 2008) to reflect on their practice, communicate with parents and colleagues, or both.

Framed Around a Faculty or School

Some initiatives have engaged groups of faculty or an entire school engaged in making teaching public. If the faculty are attempting to coordinate scholarship of teaching and learning efforts the process can be difficult to launch and sustain. Many K–12 schools have some web presence (e.g., Woodlands School, 2008) that may describe the school mission, curriculum, faculty information, and community outreach, but are oriented around issues of recruitment and information dissemination as opposed to making the school practices public. Few open windows to the rationales for faculty approaches, the development of their understandings over time, and their patterns of collaboration. One notable exception is the "Community Program" directed by LiPing Ma and Matt Ellinger. Ma and Ellinger spent 2 years working closely with a group of teachers at Slater Elementary in Mountain View, California. The group focused on the development of mathematics understanding in the teachers and the effects on their mathematics teaching (Ma, 1999), documenting their individual faculty practices, group reflections, professional development sessions led by Ma and Ellinger, and examples of faculty and student work in mathematical understandings (Lampkin, 2006).

Framed Around a Large-Scale Initiative

The examples of large-scale education-related MRT initiatives are relatively few, but there are innovative examples that might serve as inspirations for ways to organize, represent, and draw meaning from multiple MRTs. Although not explicitly representing "teaching," the Center for Digital Storytelling (2008) aims to unveil "community memory," inviting broad audiences to create individual digital stories made public on their website (see Dennis, 2008). The *Journal for Interactive Multimedia in Education* (see Burgos, 2007) describes innovative uses of multimedia *for* education but is largely text-only: it is not an immersive multimedia environment itself. *Born Magazine* is an artistic interactive literary magazine with selected pieces on topics related to teaching (e.g., Kocher & Andrews, 2001). The innovative and imaginative work done by Second Story Interactive (Johnson, 2005) expands our understandings of how museums might teach, engage audiences in learning, and represent *their* practices online.

Larger-scale initiatives explicitly devoted to teaching, learning, and education audiences include InsideWritingWorkshop.org (Noyce Foundation, 2007a, also described in this volume), an MRT developed by the Noyce Foundation's Every Child a Reader and Writer Program. InsideWriting-Workshop describes work in four classrooms and in a series of professional development workshops, all focusing on the teaching of narrative writing in elementary school. TeacherTube.com (TeacherTube, 2008) offers tools for educators to upload that enable teachers to share videos from their classrooms; further, like its model, YouTube.com, the site allows videos to be linked to others identified by the site as "similar." As of this writing it offers 379 videos linked to the keyword *algebra*, including videos sharing review worksheets, word problems, and descriptions of how to derive the quadratic equation. These numbers will surely increase as teachers, schools, parents, and communities become increasingly comfortable with granting permission for students' images and work to be posted online (Robbins, 2002).

WHOM ARE MRTS FOR? HOW ARE THEY USED?

MRTs can be used in different contexts for different audiences. They have been used in environments of preservice teacher preparation (Grossman

& Compton, 2006; Lieberman & Pointer Mace, 2008; Richert, 2006; Schultz, 2006). They have been used in graduate-level education as cases for building research methodologies and developing a case-analysis approach to teaching (Hammerness, Shulman, & Darling-Hammond, 2000) and for developing pedagogical content knowledge in practicing teachers over the long term (Noyce Foundation, 2007b; Sawyers, Fountas, Pinnell, Scharer, & Walker, 2007) and short term (Keren-Kolb & Fishman, 2006). They have been used to create and sustain networks of practitioners (Huber & Hutchings, 2005; Lieberman & Miller, 2008; Lieberman & Pointer Mace, 2008; Pointer Mace, 2008). I have yet to see examples of direct policy influences effected by MRTs, though policymakers' decisions might be transformed if their educational data included complex images of teaching and learning practices.

HOW DOES THE EMERGENCE OF MRTS CONNECT TO OTHER DEVELOPING TRADITIONS?

These varied efforts to go public with teaching and learning are evolving in tandem with broader emerging technological trends, including increasing familiarity with traditions of scholarship of teaching and learning in higher education and K–12 (Hutchings & Shulman, 1999), narrative case methods for teachers applying for National Board certification (Shulman & Sato, 2006) and teacher research (Lytle, 1997). Simultaneously, enormous online destinations like Wikipedia.org (Wikimedia Foundation, 2008), Flickr.com (Yahoo, 2008), and Delicious.com (Delicious, 2008) are inverting the process of knowledge creation and description by engaging users in co-construction of content and "folksonomic" social tagging of individual digital artifacts (Vander Wal, 2007). I don't see these as parallel initiatives. Rather, I see my own efforts with my collaborators as braiding together with these strands of knowledge creation and technological innovation. It's an exciting time to be doing this work!

DILEMMAS IN MRTS: A DIALOGUE

There is not currently one unified approach to the creation, representation, and use of MRTs. Those of us working in this fast-developing field have to address problematic issues if we want to expand the field and support its legitimacy. I'd like to close this chapter with a set of questions that shape my current thinking, ones that I extend to those whose work I've described in this chapter.

How Do People Learn to Read and Discuss MRTs?

MRTs are not the same as books, or articles, or documentary films. They don't necessarily evolve in a linear or sequential narrative, contain similar artifacts, or retain aesthetic conventions from one to the next. This makes them tricky to create and even trickier to read. If we propose to expand the use of MRTs in environments of teacher learning, we have to be prepared to make the literacies for their use explicit. One innovative way of addressing this problem was developed by Judy Shulman, who included a "Teaching Note" in the MRT she created with Elizabeth Sharkey (Shulman & Sharkey, 2006) describing how she would use the site for professional development in Jewish Education.

Who Decides If an MRT Is Any Good?

At present, there are also no accepted conventions for *vetting* MRTs. What aspects of an MRT might determine its value? The quality of the teaching or the quality of the video? The organization of the elements of the site? The narrative strength of the explanatory text? The depth of information represented? The number of questions answered? In March 2008, a meeting held at the Carnegie Foundation brought together MRT creators as a first step toward establishing standards that might be used to create some kind of expectations for the peer review of MRTs (Ellinger, 2008), but this consensus is still developing.

Who Owns an MRT?

In this litigious era, developers of MRTs need to have this conversation with all stakeholders. These stakeholders include the participants: the teacher herself and her students (and their parents, if the students are minors). But these stakeholders are in a context that may also assert control over the process and the products; the school leadership, the school district, local school boards, and policymakers may also exert influence on how teaching is to be represented. Open Knowledge Initiatives (OKI) (2008) and Creative Commons.org (Creative Commons, 2008) can help MRT developers and participants be explicit about to whom the MRT belongs and the conditions under which the MRT as a whole and its individual artifact components can be used and "remixed" (Lessig, 2006).

How Can Practicing Teachers Find the Time
to Create Their Own MRTs?

Teachers are notoriously busy people. They work long days, on weekends, and during summers to serve their student populations. We can't ask people with overscheduled calendars to add something new to their daily or weekly routine. Any attempt to engage practicing teachers in going public with their work must be embedded within their teaching. Starting small is an important part of this. We must not ask teachers to aim to document an entire school year, as inspiring as Magdalene Lampert and Deborah Ball's (1998) work may be. Instead, we can invite them to start small: Ask teachers to take digital photos of student work samples and to e-mail them to other teachers explaining how they connected to their lessons. Or invite teachers with a similar approach to literacy instruction to set up their digital camera on "movie" setting to capture a 5-minute writing conference with a student. If there's one thing I've observed about my teaching colleagues over the years, it's that they are energized by seeing each other in action and by looking closely at their students' learning. Connecting MRTs to these endeavors will help teachers see that creating an MRT is not *an addition to* teaching, it *is* teaching.

    As I'll describe in the coming chapters, my own process to invent and elaborate multimedia representations of teaching and learning has been greatly informed by many of the individuals in this present chapter. But my first chance to do this work myself was in Terry Loomis's classroom. With Loomis and her students, I learned how to *see* teaching using multimedia.

QUESTIONS FOR REFLECTION AND CONVERSATION

- What approaches to the creation of multimedia representations of teaching most resonate with you?
- Who would own a multimedia representation of your teaching practice?

Terry Loomis: Learning to See, Learning to Do

TERRY LOOMIS IS a friendly, frank teacher. Her easy smile and animated gestures speak wordlessly of her commitment to her students and to Morris School, located in a large urban school district in the San Francisco Bay Area, only a mile from where I'd begun my own teaching career. In only her 3rd year of teaching in the Spring of 2000, Loomis impressed me with her critical, self-reflective, inquiry-based approach to her linguistically diverse classroom. Her students appeared to be knowledgeable and curious about each other's home languages and cultures. She had designed some classroom activities for students to share such knowledge with each other, with plans for more such activities in the second semester of the school year. I spoke with Terry about the possibility of observing her class and interviewing her students, and she was excited to collaborate with and learn from such observations.

In January 2000, I began visiting Loomis's classroom once a week during her literacy center time. During the time I spent in her classroom, I observed that she worked reflectively and continuously to develop a curriculum that valued and responded to the linguistic diversity in her classroom, while ensuring that students developed the language and literacy skills to express themselves articulately. She prioritized communication, group work, and functional mastery of English and encouraged her students to act also as teachers. Her curriculum involved inquiry projects, which developed into opportunities for students to share their home languages and cultures with the other students in the class. Over the course of several months, I followed her students around the classroom, interviewed them at recess, and selected several to take home audio tape recorders to collect examples of their home language use. Unexpectedly, one result of the audiotape project was the decision by some students to develop their own video-based inquiry project, which they conducted with my help and presented to the class.

The teacher's name in this chapter is a pseudonym, at her request.

Together, the classroom curriculum and the students' priorities for sharing their own and learning from each other's linguistic and cultural backgrounds yielded a classroom culture in which students used the tools made available to them to document and present scenes from their lives outside of school. My own use of audiovisual media tools throughout my time in Terry's classroom connected with the students' decisions to document and share their language and culture by making short films and sharing them with their classmates. In so doing, they developed a strong sense of audience and an awareness of the implications for sharing in this way. They were empowered to address perceived curricular shortcomings by suggesting, designing, and carrying out their own cultural video inquiry projects.

THE ROLE OF MULTIMEDIA DOCUMENTATION

This was my first experience attempting to document large segments of classroom practice through multimedia. I was curious to explore how the integration of audiovisual tools allowed students to document and share their own home language use and, building upon the tradition of inquiry in the classroom, what new inquiry possibilities such audiovisual documentation presented to them. In this chapter I will describe two multimedia projects—one planned, one not—that allowed students to show their classmates the different ways in which they navigated their two languages in out-of-school settings. The projects showed the diverse ways in which students in Room 3 moved through their worlds bilingually, interacting with parents, siblings, relatives, friends, and popular culture. The students showed a real concern for the ways in which their projects would be received by their peers, and they seized the opportunity to teach each other about their lives. The planned project, the student audio interviews, revealed aspects of the students' home languages and cultures, but also uncovered the different ways in which each student approached the audiotaping task. The unplanned project, the movies created by the Spanish-speaking students, illuminated the students' own priorities for teaching their peers about their home language and culture, as well as the personal risks assumed in such a showcase.

This chapter describes both projects, including how the movie project arose out of student reflections on the audio project, and concludes with an analysis about how each project allowed students to bridge their language worlds of home and school, within the context of an inquiry-based classroom environment. Because the unfolding of these projects was so closely knit with the data yielded, and because the movie project arose unexpectedly out of the conduct of the audio project, I describe the events, perspectives, and analysis of the two media projects chronologically.

USING MEDIA TOOLS TO DOCUMENT LANGUAGE AND CULTURE

I originally conceived of the audio journal component of my study to reveal the ways in which the students were using their languages at home. I wanted to work with a large cross-section of students in the class and knew that home visits would not be feasible in the amount of time I had available. Further, I wanted to gather audio data from students whose primary languages I did not speak, the native speakers of Khmer and Vietnamese. The original goal, then, was to gather a linguistically diverse subsection of the students in Room 3, have them practice taping each other, and then send them home with one of the eight portable tape recorders belonging to the school to gather examples of their home language use. I selected six students and asked each of them to bring one friend; the students were chosen to reflect the linguistic diversity of the classroom. We met four times in the "teacher room" of the school, which served at different times of the day as a teachers' lunchroom, a staff meeting place, and a small-group workspace.

INTRODUCING THE PLANNED MULTIMEDIA PROJECT

I explained the goal of the audio project to the students, and not surprisingly, they were very excited about the prospect of taking a tape recorder home with them.

> DP: What we're going to do here is some of the stuff that I've been interested in, in language. So we're gonna talk a little bit about . . .
> JENNIFER: Language!
> DP: Language, and what language is like in families, and the ways in which you use language in the classroom, and the ways in which you use language at home. And then tomorrow, some of you will be taking home these Walkmans.
> (Most of the kids sit up straight; lots of oohing and aahing.)
> DP: And you'll be making a tape recording for me over the weekend of the kinds of ways in which you use language at home. Now, there are only eight of them, so not all of you

will take them home this weekend, but all of you will take them home at some point.

Once I was assured that students understood the goals of the project, I distributed the tape recorders, audiotapes, and batteries and asked them to practice interviewing each other. As they did so, I circulated around the teachers' room, helping students with either conceptual or technological issues. As I circulated, I noticed that the students were very excited not only about being tape-recorded, but also by playing their voices back and listening to them (Figure 3.1).

During their practice play with the tape recorders, the students began to recognize the different possibilities available to them in capturing their own and other people's language use. They capitalized on these different possibilities by adopting diverse approaches to the individual task of audio documentation. Over the course of the taping project, the students revealed different priorities for approaching the task of documenting their home language use. Some appropriated my own methodology, asking similar questions to those I had posed to them in Room 3. Others recorded their family interactions with a strong sense of the student and researcher audience with whom their tape would be shared. Some students documented extensive use of their primary languages, others none at all. The students' tapes showed how differently each student wove her or his individual strands of home language use into the classroom culture tapestry (see Pointer, 2001, for a full description of the findings).

Figure 3.1. Alex and Saroun listen back to their tape recording.

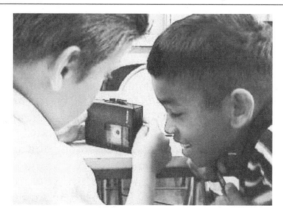

"WHY DON'T THEY CELEBRATE MEXICANS?":
AN UNEXPECTED TURN

After the students completed their home audiotaping, I debriefed with groups of students about their experiences documenting their use of multiple languages outside school. Because I had noted overlap in some of the resources recorded (radio stations, for example), I interviewed students in linguistically homogeneous groups.

During my conversation with the native-Spanish-speaking students, the students moved from appreciation of being able to use their primary language in class (Figure 3.2), to a discussion about how they wanted even more focus on their language and culture, to collectively constructing a plan of action for doing their own culture project.

> DP: How does it make you feel to speak Spanish in your class?
> DESIREE: Better, because usually we don't get a chance to speak our language.
> CARLA: It's a good thing that she lets us, but it's not enough.
> DP: Not enough?
> CARLA: That's what I think.
> DP: So what would be your recommendation?
> DESIREE: That we could learn about Mexico and stuff like that.
> DULCE: Yeah, we should learn the history of Mexico. Like when we did Black history. And we never had the Mexican history. That made me so mad.

Figure 3.2. Dulce, Carla, and Desiree discuss the use of English in their classroom.

CARLA: . . . and it makes us feel left out.

DESIREE: Um, one time, um, I was here, and you know how we celebrated, and we had a party, and we went to the Cambodian temple, and you know, on Cinco de Mayo, my family, I thought that we would do something over here. Because in my family we had a big fiesta. And everybody, you know, by where I live? They're all Spanish. They're Spanish. So we had a big party and everybody was invited? And we had fun, but I told my mom, how come we don't study about Mexicans in our school—in my class?

CARLA: I talked to my mom tons of times, and she says, "Talk to your teacher. Tell her you want to do something."

DP: And did you talk to her?

DULCE: I know that sometimes people, like, don't have money to do that stuff, like, sometimes when we're gonna have a party, and we don't have money to do that, but probably, if we didn't have money for that, then how come they had money for Cambodian New Year, to bring some storytellers for Chinese New Year, Vietnamese.

DESIREE: I think they should put it fair, because there's all kinds of different cultures over here.

DULCE: Because I'm, you know how they, the Cambodian families brought food from their culture and we ate it in class, the Mexican families could bring some food, because my *abuelita* she makes some good tacos and burritos! It's like Ms. Loomis started putting every class. Like we have Cambodian, Vietnamese, and we have more Spanish in our class. She should, um, have studies about every language but we haven't learned about our language.

DP: Do you think you should talk to your teacher about it?

DULCE and CARLA: Yes.

I was profoundly struck by the students' response to their complaints about the curriculum and not having spent enough time on studying their language and culture. They did not see it as a failing of Ms. Loomis to teach them, but instead voiced a desire to do their own project on their culture, as the Cambodian and Vietnamese students had done. The inquiry environment of the classroom empowered them to take charge of their own perceived educational needs and voice them to their teacher, with every confidence that she would support them. In the next section of this chapter, I will describe how the project that the students decided on took shape and how it allowed them to share their language and culture with the other students in their classroom.

THE UNPLANNED MULTIMEDIA PROJECT:
MAKING MOVIES TO SHARE LANGUAGE AND CULTURE

I accompanied the students back to the classroom, where Terry Loomis was assembling the other students in a line to go to lunch. The students gathered around her, talking all at once about their project ideas, and she looked at me over their heads with amusement. I explained to her that the students had been very excited about doing a project on their language and culture and that they felt that she would support them in doing it as she had with the Vietnamese and Cambodian kids, but that I also realized that it was very close to the end of the school year. I offered my support to help the students execute their project; I had materials and resources from my teaching days that I thought I might incorporate. We agreed that I would come back the following day and see who of the native-Spanish-speaking students wanted to be involved in a culture-specific project and that I would work with the students to do short (30 seconds to 2 minutes) videos on topics of their choice.

Brainstorming Project Ideas

When I returned to Morris the next day, we had arranged that I would take the native Spanish speakers who were interested in doing a special project out of the classroom for a brief meeting and brainstorm. All but one came outside to meet. I asked Desiree to explain what we'd talked about the day before that had sparked the idea to do a special project on Latino culture. Students immediately began to generate ideas that they wanted to share with their classmates.

> DULCE: El doce de diciembre . . . y el veinticuatro . . . digo! Oh! Porque, es diferente porque en vez de ser Christmas se celebra el dia de los reyes magos [The 12th of December (day of the Virgin of Guadalupe) . . . and the 24th . . . oh! Because it's different because instead of it being Christmas we celebrate the day of the Three Kings].
> MELI F.: El Dia de los Muertos [The Day of the Dead]!

The students continued to animatedly generate ideas, many of which had to do with holidays that are celebrated differently in Mexico and Central America. I asked them to think about the cultural ideas that they personally wanted to focus on and to bring in things from home that they wanted to share with their fellow students. Several students immediately thought of things they could bring and rapidly code-switched between English and Spanish as they shared their ideas with the rest of the group.

However, some students expressed concern about the way that their project would be received by the other students in the class. Although they wanted to share it with their class, they did not want a negative response.

> MELISSA: Some people, like Alton, and Brittany, they started laughing when there was an assembly and people were singing in Spanish.
> DULCE: They'll laugh! Do we laugh when they're doing it? No.
> ALEX: Pero si traemos música en español, luego nos van a decir cosas. (He sways from side to side, and drops his head, looking at the ground.) Porque no le entienden. [But if we bring music in Spanish, then they're going to say things . . . because they don't understand it.]

I asked them how they might explain their project to their classmates in a way that would elicit respect. Dulce and Alex immediately added two proactive suggestions.

> DULCE: You know, in community circle, we could, like, say something about Mexico?
> ALEX: Instead of whatever the subject is?

Several students nod in agreement. Alex continues, switching to Spanish.

> ALEX: ¿O podemos usar una canción que tiene poquito ingles y poquito español? ¡Como Ricky Martin! [We could use a song that has a little bit of English and a little bit of Spanish? Like Ricky Martin!]

He smiles and dances slightly, holding his collar and moving from right to left [Figure 3.3], and several of the girls laugh.

By intentionally selecting music for their films with cross-linguistic appeal, the students made a conscious choice to make their culture projects accessible to their diverse classroom.

Making the Movies

The following Monday, I came back to the classroom and took the students who were interested in doing the project to the teachers' room. I explained to them that they were going to do short movies about their culture, to show to their class. I said that they would be working in groups

Figure 3.3. Alex dances like Ricky Martin.

of two or three, to keep the decision-making process feasible in the 2 hours that we had to do the project.

We began by creating storyboards (Figures 3.4 and 3.5). I explained the concept of a storyboard to them and told them that in their groups, they would decide what things they wanted to share about their language and culture. Then, they would use a large piece of paper to chart the different things that they wanted to include in their story, and write the accompanying text that they would read as voiceover. I then asked the

Figure 3.4. I show the students how to do a storyboard for their movie.

Figure 3.5. Sophia and Jessica discuss their ideas for their storyboard.

students to divide themselves up into groups and begin work on their storyboards. As they worked, I circulated to ask students about their ideas. As students continued their storyboard work in groups, it became apparent that students wanted pictures of things that they did not have in their possession. At that point, several students listed items that they needed, including pictures of traditional dancing (*baile folklórico*), "la Llorona," Day of the Dead, and fireworks, just to name a few.

After the students had completed their storyboards, they had to practice reading through their text a few times (Figures 3.6 and 3.7) so that

Figure 3.6. Melissa, Natalie, and Desiree practice reading their storyboard.

Figure 3.7. Sophia and Jessica rehearse their voiceover.

their recordings would go smoothly. After each group had decided that it was ready to record its voiceovers for its movies, I took the students into the hall and videotaped them (Figures 3.8 and 3.9). They spoke assuredly and clearly, and on only one occasion did we have to reshoot the voiceover because of a student mistake. The students' voiceovers showed their versatility in approach to the task, dedication to identifying the things that they found special about their culture and wanted to share with their classmates, and their enthusiasm for doing the project.

Figure 3.8. Krizia and Alex record their voiceovers.

Figure 3.9. Carla and Dulce read from their storyboard.

GROUP ONE: KRIZIA AND ALEX

ALEX: Hola. Nos llamamos Krizia y Alex. Somos estudiantes. Vamos a hablar sobre nuestra cultura. [Hello. Our names are Krizia and Alex. We are students. We are going to talk about our culture.]

KRIZIA: Esta es la bandera mexicana y esta es la bandera salvadoreña. [This is the Mexican flag and this is the Salvadoran flag.]

ALEX: En México hay muchos arcoiris. [In Mexico, there are many rainbows.]

KRIZIA: Cuando celebramos el año nuevo tiramos cohetes. [When we celebrate the New Year, we set off fireworks.]

ALEX: En el dia de la virgen Maria, todos van a misa. [On the day of the Virgin Mary, everyone goes to mass.]

KRIZIA: En el dia de los muertos, algunas personas van a limpiar las tumbas. [On the day of the dead, some people go to clean the tombs.]

ALEX: Asi es como celebramos nuestra cultura. Adios por ahora. [That is how we celebrate our culture. Goodbye for now.] (They wave.)

GROUP TWO: DULCE AND CARLA

DULCE: Hola, nuestros nombres son Karla y Dulce Maria. En nuestra pelicula vamos a mostrarles nuestra cultura. Nuestra cultura es mexicana. (To Carla) I can't read it! . . . un dia mi familia vio a la

llorona. (Again, to Carla) Oh, that should be you! [Hello, our
names are Carla and Dulce Maria. In our film we are going to
show you our culture. Our culture is Mexican. I can't read it!
One day my family saw the Llorona. Oh, that should be you!]

KARLA: Un dia mi familia vio a la llorona. Ellos se asustaron mucho
y corrieron. [One day my family saw the Llorona. They were
very afraid and ran away.]

DULCE: Mexicanos dicen que ellos son los mejores porque los
mexicanos inventaron los tacos, las enchiladas, y agua de
orchata. Tambien inventaron muchas cosas mas. Y estoy muy
orgullosa de ser mexicana porque nosotros somos bien "cool."
(She smiles.) [Mexicans say that they are the best because
Mexicans invented tacos, enchiladas, and orchata (rice drink).
They also invented many other things. And I am very proud to
be Mexican because we are very cool.]

KARLA: En el Cinco de Mayo nosotros celebramos la guerra contra
la Francia y Pueblo. Puebla ganó. En el Dia de los Muertos,
recordamos a la gente que murio en nuestra familia. En el
doce de diciembre, nosotros celebramos el dia de la virgen
Guadalupe. [On the fifth of May we celebrate the war between
France and Puebla. Puebla won. On the Day of the Dead, we
remember the people who died in our family. On the 12th of
December we celebrate the day of the Virgin Guadalupe.]

DULCE: En Mexico, nosotros no celebramos navidad. Nosotros, en
vez de navidad, celebramos el dia de los tres reyes magos.
Ahora vamos a enseñarle musica latina. Primero, la cancion
de Shakira, "Ojos así." Esta cancion la escogimos porque tiene
una narracion en arabe. La segunda cancion es Selena y se
llama "Dondequiera que estes." Esta cancion la escogimos
porque es musica en pop, rap, y rock en español. Y tambien
Maná, "En el muelle de los santos." [In Mexico, we don't
celebrate Christmas. Instead of celebrating Christmas, we
celebrate the day of the Three Kings. Now, we are going to
teach you about Latin music. First, a song by Shakira, "Eyes
Like That." We chose this song because it has a narration
in Arabic. The second song is by Selena and is called "Wher-
ever You Are." We chose this song because it is pop, rap,
and Spanish rock. And also Maná, "In the Alley of the
Saints."]

KARLA: (unison) . . . en pop, rap, y rock en español. Y tambien
Maná, "En el muelle de los santos". [. . . pop, rap, and Spanish
rock. And also Maná, "In the Alley of the Saints."]

GROUP THREE: NATALIE, DESIREE, AND MELISSA

UNISON: Hola. Nos llamamos [Hello. Our names are]

NATALIE: Natalie . . .

DESIREE: Desiree . . .

MELISSA: y Melissa.

NATALIE: Nosotras queremos decirles de unas historias espantosas de nuestra cultura. [We want to tell you about some scary stories from our culture.]

MELISSA: Como la Llorona. Es una historia de una señora que murió hace muchos años y siempre anda por las noches en México para agarrar a sus hijos. [Like the Llorona. It's a story about a woman who died long ago and always comes out at night in Mexico to grab children.]

DESIREE: We also want to tell you about Navidad and how God was born. For example, a angel came up to the . . . Virgin Maria and said, "Please be Jesus' mother."

NATALIE: Queremos decirles de las comidas especiales. Como el pozole y las enchiladas y un jugo delicioso la jamaica en el verano. [We want to tell you about some special foods. Like pozole and enchiladas and a delicious juice—the "jamaica"—in the summer.]

MELISSA: Queremos decirles del Cinco de Mayo. Vienen personas a cantar. [We want to tell you about the 5th of May. People come to sing.]

DESIREE: And we also want to tell you about the Day of the Dead. The prettiest . . . (she hesitates, brings her hands up and lays them against her cheeks) occasion.

NATALIE: La virgen de Guadalupe es la santa patrona de México. [The Virgin of Guadalupe is the patron saint of Mexico.]

MELISSA: Queremos decirles que hay muchas . . . clases de ropa. [We want to tell you that there are many different kinds of clothes.]

DESIREE: The Last Supper is a very important thing for México.

NATALIE: En México hay preciosos flores, como una que hace un jugo delicioso que se llama la jamaica. [In Mexico there are beautiful flowers, like one that makes a delicious juice that is called the "jamaica."]

MELISSA: Queremos decirles lo especial de hablar español. Es que México tiene muchas historias especiales. [We want to tell you about how special it is to speak Spanish. It's that Mexico has many special stories.]

Unison: We just told you about our culture. We hope you can tell us about yours! (They wave.)

GROUP FOUR: JESSICA, SOPHIA, AND GIOVANNA

Unison: Hi, our names are
Jessica: Jessica . . .
Sophia: Sophia . . .
Giovanna: and Giovanna. We celebrate Cinco de Mayo. We celebrate Christmas. We go to church every Sunday.
Jessica: We go to catechism to learn about God and how he survived in the sand. We make our first communion. Then we make our first communion. Mexico is our country. Almost everyone there believes in God.
Sophia: We celebrate the New Year by cooking tacos, also praying. We sing Mexican songs.
Jessica: Some people in Mexico believe in the Easter bunny. (She smiles.) To speak Spanish, it is important because I am forgetting it.
Sophia: For me to speak Spanish is important and I'm scared I'll forget to speak it. I also want to write it.
Unison: We hope you like our film.

Each group prioritized different things about their cultural traditions—different holidays, different legends, different religious observances—but all spoke with pride about the things that made their shared cultural experiences special. Unfortunately, we only had a small amount of time to execute the projects and a limited amount of disk space onto which to capture the digital video; otherwise the students would have been able to develop longer narratives.

After the students had recorded their voiceovers, I took home their storyboards, the materials they'd brought from home to include in their movies, their written subtitles, and the list of photos to retrieve from the Internet. I used a Macintosh PowerBook G3 with a 233mHz processor and the freeware program iMovie to create the movies. I then exported the students' finished films and the "making of" film to 8mm tape and transferred them to VHS, so that we could play them back for the whole class.

Room 3 Film Festival: Sharing the Movies

The following Monday (in the last week of school), I brought the tape to Room 3, along with refreshments for the class to thank them for their participation in my research. Terry Loomis asked the students who had participated in making the movies to come to the front of the room and talk about what they had done, while I set up the VCR. Students talked about bringing music and pictures from home, about writing their family stories, and about listing resources from the Internet. They spoke a bit hesitantly, because they hadn't even seen the finished products yet. Once we had the VCR functioning, the students sat back down and the whole class watched the movies. All together they totaled about 5 minutes of film, but the students were transfixed the whole time. After the films were finished, Terry asked the class if they had any comments or questions. Immediately, several hands shot up.

> EUGENE: That was very good!
> STEPHEN: I like how you did that.

Although the students had articulated fears about the way that their project would be received by their peers, there was not a single snicker in the room. After the movie presentation, the students spoke animatedly with their table groups about the experience of making the movies.

LEARNING FROM THE UNEXPECTED:
THE POTENTIAL FOR MULTIMEDIA IN THE CLASSROOM

I did not originally intend to run a digital video project with students as part of my research in Terry Loomis's room; when the students articulated their desire to do a project on their culture, it seemed a logical extension of their work with the audiotapes. Students demonstrated a profound sense of audience, illustrated by their voiced concerns and discussions about other students' reactions to their projects. The fact that students felt so comfortable sharing their home experiences emerged from the classroom environment of respect and inquiry. Although these students lived their school lives at the crossroads of many potent social dynamics—poverty, violence, racism, and anti-immigrant sentiment, to name just a few—they illustrated through their movies a vital, passionate desire to give creative voice to their lives and experiences.

Terry Loomis's students were my research subjects, but they were also among my best teachers of the use of multimedia tools to capture classroom life. I had to be open to the students' ideas about sharing their cultural knowledge and expertise, give them a chance to apply these ideas with the multimedia tools available, and develop an outcome project to allow them to make their ideas public. While this collaboration did not result in a website, as the rest of the chapters in this book describe, it powerfully illustrated to me how invisible the layers of classroom life can be, even to those looking closely. An active solicitation of multiple voices and perspectives greatly expanded my understanding of how Terry Loomis's students viewed their cultural identities and classroom diversity.

QUESTIONS FOR REFLECTION AND CONVERSATION

- How might you engage your students in collaborative cultural inquiry?
- What kinds of multimedia documentation might your students be able to generate?
- What pieces of your classroom cultural "tapestry" would you want to make public?

Yvonne Divans Hutchinson:
Capturing the Complexity
of Experienced Teaching Practice

Y VONNE DIVANS HUTCHINSON is an unlikely bootlegger. Tall and elegant, she walks the halls of King/Drew Medical Magnet High School with the commanding grace and warmth accrued over 40 years spent teaching high school English. Her ninth-grade English class at King/Drew provides a daily counterpoint to the stereotypes about urban African American and Latino teenagers perpetuated by popular media. Hutchinson's students are eloquent, insightful, playful, and passionate about discussing the texts in her class, whether it be a memoir of a jazz musician growing up in the Jim Crow South, or the combative intergroup insults of *Romeo and Juliet*. As mentioned in Chapter 1, Yvonne Hutchinson herself is well known throughout the Los Angeles Unified School District and beyond for her success with students and her work as a mentor to other teachers. She regularly hosts student teachers and field students in her classroom and has informal and formal mentorships with novice and veteran colleagues. She works as a teacher educator at various university campuses in the Los Angeles area and is a teacher consultant for the National Writing Project. Mike Rose, the UCLA writer and scholar, vividly described her classroom in the opening chapter of his book *Possible Lives*:

> All day long, Yvonne Divans Hutchinson demonstrated, encouraged, celebrated and guided students through an active and critical reading process that undercut the common perception that reading simply involved the decoding of words, that print had single, basic meanings that students had to decipher quietly and store away. She had students write in a "reading journal" a dialogue between themselves and the author of whatever book they were currently reading, agreeing, disagreeing, sympathizing, questioning—engaging the ideas in the pages. (1995, p. 8)

It might not surprise you, then, that many teachers wanted to see Hutchinson's classroom in action.

After Hutchinson completed her certification from the National Board for Professional Teaching Standards (NBPTS), she started entertaining a new kind of request: colleagues wanted to see her National Board videotape. The National Board portfolio submission process includes two "classroom-based entries that require video recordings of interactions between you and your students" (NBPTS, 2008b). Hutchinson had chosen to include video of her students animatedly discussing a selection of literature. In that video, Hutchinson plays the role of guide and facilitator. The students' contributions direct the flow of the discussion while Hutchinson literally positions herself behind the students, only occasionally chiming in. The students recognize each other's turns to talk and the majority of the students' voices are heard. This particular alchemy can be very difficult to get going in any classroom, so after word spread that Hutchinson's students were accomplished discussants of literature, teachers she'd never met began to contact her to ask to see the video—which is where the bootlegging dilemma comes in. After teachers submit their portfolios to the National Board for assessment, the materials become the property of NBPTS. Hutchinson was unable to share this particular video with her colleagues.

Happily, generative teaching rarely only happens once. At the time, Hutchinson was a fellow in the Carnegie Academy for the Scholarship of Teaching and Learning (CASTL). Her Scholarship of Teaching project involved considering how she was working to get students who were very comfortable speaking to align their oral contributions more closely with the literature. A published poet as well as teacher, Hutchinson developed vivid language to describe this effort and gave her project the evocative title "From Shuckin' and Jivin' to Academic Discourse." In conversation with me one day during the CASTL residency at the Carnegie Foundation, she remarked that it would be wonderful to help people understand how "academic discourse" was enacted in her classroom and described the multiple requests she had received for copies of her NBPTS videotape. We realized we had an opportunity to capture her practice in a way that already anticipated the interests and needs of a particular audience. We planned for me to fly down to Los Angeles and document one day of her teaching, and we'd see where things went from there. We weren't sure whether we would make a DVD of the day that she could distribute to interested colleagues, or a website showing more than just video of her teaching. Once we had collected some artifacts and footage of her practice, we could have that conversation.

GOING PUBLIC WITH HUTCHINSON'S CLASS:
INVENTING THE "CLASS ANATOMY"

On an early day in June 2002, I packed a portable scanner, two video cameras and tripods, lapel and table microphones, my laptop, and a comfortable pair of clogs. I arrived at King/Drew about an hour before the beginning of classes. The building itself stands in stark contrast to the surrounding neighborhood. Built in the late 1990s, the glass, chrome, and brick architecture echoes the adjoining King/Drew Hospital, in which students are expected to become involved as interns during their high school career. Hutchinson began teaching at King/Drew after teaching English for many years in nearby Markham middle school.

Hutchinson's classroom is full of vibrant colors, images of African American and Latino leaders alongside inspirational quotes, and books lining every wall of the classroom. On the day I visited her classroom, her students were seated at two rectangular blocks of desks facing each other, with an aisle down the middle. On other days, I came to know, they would sit in a circle, or push the desks along the walls, depending on the day's focus.

CONTENT FOCUS: FACILITATING A DISCUSSION OF A MEMOIR

That day, Hutchinson's students were discussing *A Call to Assembly*, a memoir written by the jazz musician and Yale School of Music faculty member Willie Ruff (1991). In the book, Ruff tells the story of his upbringing in Jim Crow Alabama, his infatuation with music and development as a musician, and his collaborations with some of the most renowned and influential jazz figures of the day. The excerpt Hutchinson had selected for that day involved Ruff's first experience as a youth hearing the word *nigger* in his presence. Ruff was working for a Mr. Steele, a local shoe salesman who also employed a young deaf man named Smitty. Already in love with sound and music, and fascinated by the idea that this young person could communicate without hearing, Ruff worked obsessively to learn the sign language used between employer and employee. But as this excerpt illustrates, his love for sign language leads him into confrontation with his employer:

> One day at the shoeshop, I was in a conversation with Smitty and he was having trouble reading one of my signs. Though I thought I had it right, I obviously was faltering somewhere with a sign involving a complicated movement of the right fist. Mr. Steele, seeing my meaning and my problem right away, interrupted. "Naw, boy!" he said. "Your problem is you got to

hold that fist up like this." I held it up. "No! Hold it like this: just like you gonna hit a nigger." I went cold. The color of deep red began crowding my vision, and an anger welled up in me that choked off my breath. (p. 64)

In the remainder of the chapter, Ruff returns home, where his grandmother Mama Minnie admonishes him to "stoop to conquer" and return to work. After some consideration, Ruff realizes that he cannot do so:

I knew if I touched that apron something within me would die. . . . I knew I'd lost my chance for learning more in my beloved sign language, but in the bargain I'd got in touch with a part of myself I'd not known before: the part I could always rely on to let me know just how far I was willing to stoop to conquer just to "get along" in Mama Minnie's hard ol' world. (p. 66)

Willie Ruff's memoir is not a staple of ninth-grade English curricula, but its inclusion in Hutchinson's syllabus is a result of her quest to find texts that resonate with her students as well as speaking to "universal human concerns" of dignity, empathy, creativity, equity, and identity. (See Hutchinson, 1998, for a description of other literary sources used in this effort.)

PRACTITIONER GOALS

In our videotaped conversations that morning before school, Yvonne Hutchinson explained that she wanted her students to engage in conversation about these themes in the first part of her class:

First of all, I engaged them with the anticipation guide, so they would be thinking about the issues that are present in the text itself: taking the ideas beyond the text, and also at the same time to appreciate the features of the text. They have as an assignment to formulate some questions about the text themselves. The anticipation guide gets them thinking about issues, all of which are embedded in the text. I'm hoping that they will make their own meaning of this text, that is rich enough, to invite discussion on all kinds of levels about the text itself, but even more importantly, about the implications about what it says about *them*, about the social issues involved. I hope that they will find it informative in terms of looking at social issues "back in the day" (as they call it) and the relevance to today. Specifically, they look at the use of the "n-word," the pejorative, in terms of what it indicates about attitudes, and what it indicates about the human condition.

I followed up these remarks by asking Yvonne to reflect about the larger context in which this piece of literature was situated. Her response connected Ruff's memoir to larger "universal truths" that she hoped would be instilled in her students as "habits of mind" they could carry with them far beyond her ninth-grade English class.

> It's a piece about an African American boy, but it's a piece about people that I think all the children can relate to, and especially our children, being Black and Brown, being involved in situations where their dignity or intelligence is called into question. To get them involved in that conversation, one of the hallmarks of the class is always to be sensitive to the needs of others and always be sensitive to the fact that, yes, we have differences, but we also have some commonalities. There are some universal truths that we can explore. These habits of mind are important, because you are going to examine issues that are relevant to your life, relevant to being part of this society, and you're also going to engage in the kind of inquiry, and thinking, and reading, and writing, and discussion, that elevate you in terms of your ability to critically analyze situations, make decisions, and interact with other people.

Hutchinson's school practices block scheduling, so she meets with her students for 2-hour instructional periods. Her 25 ninth graders entered her classroom, all dressed in the school uniform of black pants and a white polo shirt, many wearing a black and gold King/Drew sweatshirt. They greeted her with calls of "Hi, Ms. Hutch!" and found their desks. They had been told about my visit in advance and many said a courteous "Hello" or "Welcome" as they made their way into the room. Hutchinson introduced me as Dr. Pointer Mace and asked me to tell the students a little about myself, about my teaching background, as well as where I'd attended college and graduate school. College attendance is much higher among King/Drew's students than the average in LAUSD, in part because "Ms. Hutch" and her colleagues explicitly address how to make the dream a reality and invite all visitors to their classrooms to talk about their postsecondary education.

DOCUMENTATION OF THE CLASS PERIOD

I positioned one videocamera on a tripod in a corner of the room, facing a block of students' desks. The other camera I carried with me at my side, monitor open and facing up so that I could see what I was doing without pointing a camera directly into anyone's face. I walked around the perimeter of the classroom and took still photographs of the walls to give audiences a sense of the space.

Class Scribe Report

Hutchinson opened the class by inviting a student named DJ to give the daily "class scribe report." Each day, Hutchinson asks a student to take notes on the day's events and present them the following day. This routine relies on the student's powers of observation, reportage, and public speaking. That day, DJ animatedly related the previous day's events. I record his remarks here in their entirety because he paints a vivid, succinct portrait of life in "Ms. Hutch's" room:

> Hello. My name is DJ and I was class scribe for June 4, 2002. As I walked into the classroom, I realized Ms. Hutch gave us a paper called "A Call to Assembly Reading Response." Not following our usual routine, we didn't do SSR [Sustained Silent Reading]. Instead, she told us to pull out our anticipation guide. As the room drew quiet, I saw that people were trying to complete their work. She told us to get in groups of two. Everyone didn't know who to pick as their partners, so Ms. Hutch brought it upon herself to match everyone up together. We had to make a, quote-unquote, "Soul Train Line" so we formed one. Everyone stood across from each other, so everyone got matched up. It ended up that LaQuida and Rahima got paired up, and Ms. Hutch knew what was going to happen, so they paired up with someone else. It got to Ashley and Van. Ms. Hutch began to think, and Van said, "That's not my friend!" Ashley said, "That *is* my friend!" So Ms. Hutch paired them up with different people also. We all *knew* why Van said she wasn't his friend! After that, the line came to me. I was honored by having a partner as intelligent as Erika Cordoba. We discussed issues such as "Honor thy father and thy mother" and "No one can be oppressed without their consent." We were confused about number 9. Ms. Hutch then told us to move our tables into a circle. Everyone piled up against each other so Ms. Hutch told us to spread out. We began with Chris Cordoba, and she spoke on number 5. After Chris Cordoba spoke her part, I then rose my hand. We then discussed number 8, "Honor thy father and thy mother." Kristin then said she agrees and disagrees with that statement. She said she agrees, because you always need to respect

your parents, but if you feel they're wrong, you need to let them know without yelling and fussing. Van and I agreed with Kristin. Andrea then said that she agrees with us also. She replied by saying if we came up to them respectfully, and come to them as an adult, then they will look at us as their equal. After Andrea spoke, Ms. Hutch saw that we were running out of time, so she asked if anyone had a number to discuss. Tiffany said she wanted to do number 2, which had to do with the n-word. Van agreed. Ms. Hutch then began to discuss our homework. She passed us some papers which was for a story called "A Call to Assembly." She told us to mark it up and to do levels of questions on them. I said that I didn't remember the levels of questions, so Ms. Hutch gave us the old papers with the levels of questions. She began to describe them. She was interrupted by the bell. Ms. Hutch asked a couple of students to stay after school on Wednesday. Ms. Hutch dismissed the class. Respectfully submitted, Dejean.

Hutchinson invited DJ's fellow students to contribute their comments on his scribe report and called his attention to his small grammatical error by asking him if one says "raised" or "rose" one's hand. She then addressed the entire class and said that, as they'd done the day before, they would discuss some of the same issues, but with the added task of (re)considering their viewpoints from the prior discussion in light of the Ruff excerpt.

Small-Group Discussions

Calling back to DJ's gentle teasing of the two students who had tried to get paired together by claiming that they were *not* friends, Hutchinson invited the class to divide up into discussion groups:

> I want you to find someone who is different from you in some aspect—race, gender, ethnicity—who is not, dare I say this, your friend. [Here, she smiled and reached out to touch Van's shoulder.] Well, not that the person's not your friend, but not part of your "clique" outside of class. I want you to find someone with whom you are going to share your anticipation guide, and discuss those issues that resonate with you or seem most important to you. Let this be an exchange, a conversation. Keep your paper. Read what you wrote, feel free to expound upon it or to elaborate further or to ask questions of each other, and exchange ideas. Move to a place that gives you enough space to face each other, but not to be so

close that your conversation would interfere. All right. Freedom of choice, here.

The students moved into groups of twos and threes and proceeded to stand facing each other and engage in a discussion of the text. Because of the small size of the classroom and the students' comfort level in talking this way, the noise level of the room increased, so I moved closely to various groups to be able to adequately record their voices. Each shared his or her stance on the position statements in the anticipation guide:

1. A person deserves to be treated with respect regardless of her/his race, creed, color, or station in life.
2. Historically the word *nigger* is a racist term that is unacceptable under any circumstances.
3. I use the word *nigger* in my conversation with family and friends.
4. As Eleanor Roosevelt once said, "No one can make you feel inferior without your consent."
5. A poor person who needs to work should obey the wishes of her/his employer even though it conflicts with her/his beliefs or violates the person's sense of dignity and self-esteem.
6. It is possible to love/care about a person of a different race.
7. Black people often had no real power to fight against racism and the "Jim Crow" system "back in the day."
8. A child should always obey the commandment "Honor thy father and thy mother," even if she/he thinks the parent/guardian is wrong.

After 10 minutes of small-group conversation, Hutchinson invited the students back to their seats and described her stipulations for group discourse: that the students recognize each other's turn to speak, that the more vocal students not dominate, and that the more reticent students not allow themselves to be silenced.

Whole-Group Discussion

The whole-group discussion built from the text to a wide-ranging conversation about race, social change, the use of offensive language to include and exclude, the futility of (or hope for) national leadership by people of color, and many other "universal human concerns." Hutchinson stood at the perimeter of the desks and intervened periodically to return students to the Ruff text. One student, Tiffany, pointed out that by Ruff's signing, "I quit," he had pointedly rejected the teachings of the employer, and

Hutchinson connected this insight with an opportunity to get a more quiet student to participate:

> TIFFANY: The thing that struck me, like when I read this part here, on page 68, was, that instead of saying it out loud, "I quit," he *signed* it to him. It's like he was using what he had gotten from him and given it back to him.
>
> HUTCHINSON: Oh, wow, that's great!
>
> TIFFANY: It was like an insult to give *back* to him. Because he got it from him, so he's throwing it back in his face.
>
> HUTCHINSON: I want to ask . . .
>
> KRISTIN: That was *nice.*
>
> HUTCHINSON (walking up to Ashlynn, resting her hands on her shoulders): I want to ask you, because you do sign language, you said you studied sign language. Could you sign that for us?
>
> VAN: No.
>
> HUTCHINSON: . . . "I quit?" . . . Van, stop! Could you? Okay. Help her, Tiffany. Read that description.
>
> (Ashlynn is smiling, waving her hand as if to decline to share.)
>
> HUTCHINSON: Read the description. Can you do it for us? Stand up so the camera can . . .
>
> ASHLYNN: I'm fine.
>
> HUTCHINSON: You don't want to stand up? Okay. Because everybody needs to see you! Come stand by me.
>
> (Cross talk as Ashlynn gets up from her seat and walks to stand next to Hutchinson, who places her arm around her shoulders.)
>
> HUTCHINSON: I like that, I like that. That's insightful. That what he got from him, he gave it *back* to him. He threw it back at him.
>
> TIFFANY: He was like, rejecting the gift, like, if somebody gives you something, and you find it offensive, you throw it back in their face.
>
> KRISTIN: It was like a stolen item! It was like he stole something and gave it to him as a gift!
>
> HUTCHINSON: Okay, so let's see. Read the description. You gonna sign for us?
>
> (Ashlynn nods, smiling shyly.)
>
> TIFFANY: "All I could think to do, when I recovered a bit, was to rip off my apron, make a fist with my right hand, with the little finger up, and move it toward my chest, the sign for '*I*'. Then, placing the first two fingers of my right hand in my left hand, immediately snatching the two fingers out again, I signed 'I quit,' and was out the door."

Figure 4.1. Ashlynn signs "I quit" for the class.

(Ashlynn signs along with Tiffany's readaloud, then repeats the
    sign for "I quit" [Figure 4.1] and returns to her seat, ap-
    plauded by the class.)
HUTCHINSON: Wow.
KRISTIN: That was *nice*!

This vignette illustrates many of the key elements of Hutchinson's approach
to discussion: her careful selection of texts that resonate powerfully with
the concerns of her students; the development of a discourse community
in which students are expected to actively participate, make explicit reference to the text, and assert articulate responses to its themes; the role of
the teacher as a facilitator of dialogue, building on her knowledge of students' expertise to draw out less vocal students; and the idea that the
understanding of these "universal human concerns" is constructed and
advanced by the group.

After school, Hutchinson met with a group of students and asked them
to describe her expectations for them and their experiences of her class.
DJ and Tiffany drew connections between Hutchinson's goals for integrating the class, the text itself, and their futures in the "real world":

DJ: Well, Ms. Hutch has always taught us to be so diverse. When
     we group up, she makes sure we don't do it with the same
     race and same gender, for the simple fact that you'd probably
     be getting the same views, of the same kind of people. So she
     likes to let us know, well, you're a different race from him, or

you're a different race than her, so why don't you guys match up and share, possibly, your different views on different things that she gives us. And today, as you could see, everybody—this isn't just us—all of us, that have grown in Ms. Hutch. As you could see, most of the students were ready to give their knowledge and what they felt, and their opinions on every-thing. That's just a beautiful thing about Ms. Hutch's class.

TIFFANY: Also, when she diversifies the room, it seems like she's preparing us for the real world, because the real world isn't just one kind of people, speaking one language, and doing one thing with the same ideas. Because if it was, the world would just repeat itself over and over. Sometimes I do notice repetitions, like in world history, like things happen over and over, but it would be just a constant cycle, and happen exactly the same way, because there would be no new ideas. No inventions would be created. We have to learn to work with people that are different from us, too. It's preparing us for working, because sometimes you're not going to like the people that you have to work with at your job, but you can't go and quit your job just because you don't like the people that you have to work with. Sometimes, you have to learn to just deal with things like that.

Hutchinson is explicit with the students about her rationales for approach-ing instruction the way that she does; the students are thus able to articu-late how this approach will help them now and into the future.

Reflection on Artifacts Gathered

I returned home that evening energized by Hutchinson and her students, and immediately digitized the Digital8 and MiniDV tapes using iMovie, and burned them to DVDs to send to Hutchinson. I asked her to watch the entire class session and to jot down excerpts that she thought would help audiences unfamiliar with her classroom grasp some of the sig-nature features of her discussion pedagogy. She responded by identify-ing the time codes of six clips representing her preinstruction reflection, class opening, explication of the day's task, small-group discussion, large-group discussion, and student group interview. We discussed how these elements of an instructional event—planning and reflection, intro-duction, independent work, group work, closure, and reflection—are present in many other teachers' classrooms. By identifying these ele-ments, Hutchinson had articulated the "anatomy" of her practice for others to learn from.

CREATING A MULTIMEDIA REPRESENTATION
OF HUTCHINSON'S TEACHING

But an anatomy is not just a collection of components. An anatomy depends on an articulation of the structure—the relationship between the components and their place in the larger system. Hutchinson and I reflected together that any website representation of these individual moments should introduce them together, as parts of a composite whole. My initial mockup, using the HTML authoring program Dreamweaver, arranged Hutchinson's clips underneath a brief introduction to Yvonne and a list of the related artifacts from her class. The artifacts we included in our original mockup were the reading response prompt used by students on that day, the anticipation guide, a pair of documents relating to Hutchinson's reading instruction "Thinking with Text" and "Informal Reading Assessment," and Hutchinson's reflections on the website creation process. Part of our goal in creating Hutchinson's website in this modular way was to serve as a template for the Carnegie Foundation KEEP tool (Carnegie Foundation, 2008a), still in development at the time. By creating a website composed of modular "boxes," my colleagues at the Carnegie Foundation Knowledge Media Lab hoped to create a prototype of a way for scholars to upload individual artifacts of practice, describe them, and arrange them dynamically on a public webpage.

After our original draft of the website was uploaded, Hutchinson shared the link with her CASTL K–12 colleagues as well as interested teacher educators who hoped to use her website in their courses. One of this group, Pam Grossman, wanted to use the site in her graduate education courses at Stanford University and immediately spoke with Hutchinson. That following academic year, Pam experimented with using the site in a research seminar as one of several her students might elect to study for a case analysis. I met with several of Grossman's students to learn about the insights into teaching that the site afforded them. Many of these graduate students had at least a few years of teaching practice. Interestingly, when I spoke with them, they mentioned that they were simultaneously inspired and disheartened by viewing Hutchinson's practice. They found her facilitated discussion complex, far-reaching, and dauntingly impressive; they found her students brilliant and exceptional. They thought that Hutchinson's 40 years of teaching practice had resulted in some measure of professional perfection that felt remote and inaccessible to them. They had very little sense of how she had constructed these practices over time, how she had supported these students throughout nearly an entire school year to develop their own discussion competence, and how her own motives and rationale connected to the class session we'd documented. In short, they lacked a sense of context and process.

Pam and Yvonne met at Carnegie to discuss what elements might enrich audiences' understandings of her practice. Hutchinson, herself an experienced mentor to novice teachers, immediately grasped the dilemma: that accomplished practice often seems "magical" to beginners. The suite of techniques that veteran teachers employ during a given instructional event seem so effortless that they approach invisibility, but they are still there. Hutchinson needed to make these strategies visible.

She arranged for a colleague to videotape some of her class discussions at the beginning of the following year, to show how she provides a great deal more structure for student participation, even to the extent of scripting student "stock responses." She added a document to her website's supporting materials titled "Strategies for Supporting Literate Discourse in the Classroom," listing some of these stock responses. We added some examples of students' work, as well as a narrative about Hutchinson's teaching context and her student population. Our mutual goal was to reflect that complexity in her teaching practice without overwhelming audiences, without her practice seeming flawless and inaccessible. We developed a set of questions from Pam's students and I used those to interview Yvonne about the underpinnings of her practice. We included this entire interview on the website, as well as pulling out a clip from it titled "What Audiences Should Know About Yvonne's Teaching, and Her Journey to Develop This Approach." In the clip, Hutchinson connects the teaching events captured on that day with her larger goals for students' engagement with literature and larger issues of identity, society, and justice:

> Being part of traditionally oppressed groups of people, I think it is incumbent upon me as a teacher to give kids a sense of themselves, not only as people, but as part of this society. To understand those things that militate against them as well as those that they can take advantage of. One of the things that I think that teachers, new teachers, should know is that, yes, you have material, you have content, you have text, you have whatever your medium is to bring the knowledge (or to help students to acquire knowledge, as I like to think of it)—to acquire knowledge, to learn to think and to be, that aside from the page, or the material, or the story, or the document, that they have to take those little black and white marks into themselves, internalize it, and add it to their own development as human beings. We always have, as part of our

reading or contemplation of any material, movies, anything, the whole idea of taking it beyond just what it says on the page, into "What does it mean?" "Why does it matter?" and "What can I take away from this that is going to contribute to my growth?"

As Hutchinson explains in her brief professional and biographical statement "Where I Began/Where I Begin," she has had a lifelong love affair with literature. At the end of Toni Morrison's *Beloved* (1987), the character Paul D says, "She is a friend of my mind . . . The pieces I am, she gather them and give them back to me in all the right order." Hutchinson drew from this quotation to illustrate how she views her role as teacher in the title of her website, "A Friend of Their Minds" (Figure 4.2). By going public with her teaching, Hutchinson extends the circle of "friends" to encompass those not only inside her classroom but also far beyond.

HOW HUTCHINSON'S PRACTICE CAN BE USED
FOR TEACHER LEARNING AND DEVELOPMENT

I have described how Pam Grossman collaborated with Hutchinson in the early development and refinement of her website. But many other educators have used Hutchinson's work for teacher learning in their contexts. Her teaching is not just a case of one thing; good teachers serve their students' needs in many ways simultaneously.

Content Area Connection: Pam Grossman

In the years since her early role in providing feedback on the draft version of the site, Grossman has continued to refine her own use of Hutchinson's site for preservice teacher education and doctoral student research. In particular, Grossman and her colleague Christa Compton created a website (Grossman & Compton, 2006) in which they describe a multipartite assignment for their Secondary English Methods course. Grossman and Compton invite their students to work in pairs to investigate particular questions about Hutchinson's site, such as "What is the role of the anticipation guide before and during the class discussion?" and "Who speaks? How often? What does Hutchinson do to encourage everyone's participation?" The pairs compile evidence from the website for their responses to these questions and then divide into two groups to present the evidence to their fellow students by facilitating a discussion on their question. Grossman and Compton's students are then asked to try out one or more of the strategies identified in Hutchinson's practice in their own field placements, and

Figure 4.2. Screen shot of Yvonne Divans Hutchinson's MRT.

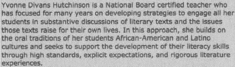

A Friend of Their Minds: Capitalizing on the Oral Tradition of My African
American Students
CLASS ANATOMY

YVONNE DIVANS HUTCHINSON
KING-DREW MEDICAL MAGNET SCHOOL
LOS ANGELES, CA

Yvonne Divans Hutchinson is a National Board certified teacher who has focused for many years on developing strategies to engage all her students in substantive discussions of literary texts and the issues those texts raise for their own lives. In this approach, she builds on the oral traditions of her students African-American and Latino cultures and seeks to support the development of their literacy skills through high standards, explicit expectations, and rigorous literature experiences.

Her online "class anatomy"- a documentation and analysis of one instructional period - juxtaposes video clips with commentary and samples of classroom documents. In the video clips, Hutchinson reflects on her expectations for the class, a student orally presents the "class scribe" notes from the previous day, the students engage in small group and large group discussion about a racially charged literary selection that had been assigned the night before, and after the class, four students reflect on their experiences in Hutchinson's classroom, and how her rigorous approach and emphasis on dialogue and diversity prepares them for other academic work.

Context and Reflections

1. Thinking with Text
2. Project Snapshot
3. Teaching Context: School and Students
4. Video: What audiences of this work should know about Yvonne's teaching, and her journey to develop this approach.
5. Narrative: Where I Began/ Where I Begin

Materials and Strategies

1. Strategies for Promoting Literate Discourse
2. Question-Answer Relationships • Student Response Sample
3. Anticipation Guide
4. Reading Response Prompt
5. Class Scribe Prompt • Class Scribe Writing Sample
6. Informal Reading Assessment

Video:
Entire class session (2 hours)
Entire reflective interview (1 hour)

How they got here:
The beginning of the school year
<<<<

Class Anatomy Timeline

Class Session: June 2002

Where they went next:
The following school year
>>>>

1. Setting Goals for the Class Session	2. Describing the Previous Day's Work	3. Engaging in Small Group Discussion

YDH tells what she expects to see as evidence of oral discourse as students discuss a memoir by Willie Ruff, "A Call to Assembly." . (4:00)	DJ, class scribe for the previous day, delivers his lively and humorous narrative of the class activities for that day. At the end of the report, his peers evaluate both the report and his delivery. Daily class scribe reports and related instructional materials or handouts are kept in a Class Notebook in the classroom. (3:03) (View the Class Scribe Prompt, or another student's Class Scribe Writing Sample)	Responding to teacher's directions to honor diversity in their choices of discussion partners, students meet in duos or trios to share their responses to the Anticipation Guide for "A Call to Assembly." (6:03)
4. Connecting to Larger Societal Issues	5. Making Explicit Reference to the Text	6. Reflecting on the Impact of Diversity, Rigor, and Discourse

Andrea speaks passionately about leaders from African American and Hispanic communities and the difficulties of effecting change. She ends her talk with an indictment of Black and Hispanic gangs and the diviseness among (and between) the two racial groups. (3:41)	Gladis begins the discussion of a pivotal moment in the text, questioning the use of the perjorative "N" word. Tiffany shows discernment in her analysis of the ten year old Ruff's motive in quitting his job. Other students voice their ideas, and the conversation culminates with Ashlan sharing her knowledge of sign language. (3:41)	Dejean, Andrea, Tiffany reveal how the requirement to honor diversity in their classroom interactions not only broadened their perspective, but resulted in new friendships. (1:44)

finally the students reflect on what it took for them to adapt the strategies to their particular contexts. On the site, Grossman and Compton's students make several insights. One reported success using Hutchinson's strategies for getting students to participate and that "the one student who had never, ever, ever spoken, spoke—it was a real victory!" Another observed that in trying to get his own discussion going he realized "how much preparation needs to go into it. You can't just sort of show up and it sort of *happens*. Hutchinson obviously does so many specific things in order to reach that point where it can happen, and sort of seem like magic. Behind the scenes there's so much more." Still another of Grossman's students even successfully sought out a teaching position at King/Drew and is now one of Hutchinson's colleagues. The impact on these students from digging under the surface of practices that can seem "magical" is considerable.

Cross-Curricular Connection: Gloria Ladson-Billings

Gloria Ladson-Billings is a professor of education at the University of Wisconsin at Madison and the author of the acclaimed book *The Dreamkeepers: Successful Teachers of African American Children* (1997). Hutchinson's MRT includes several quotes from *Dreamkeepers*, and she considers Ladson-Billings an important influence on her work serving "black and brown" children in an urban setting. Ladson-Billings came to know Hutchinson's work when they participated on the same panel presentation at a conference for the National Council of Teachers of English in 2004 and subsequently began integrating Hutchinson's work into a course for preservice teachers in middle school social studies. Like Pam Grossman, Ladson-Billings uses the site as an illustration of how a teacher can subvert the traditional "Ping-Pong" style of classroom discussion, where each student response is directed to the teacher, who then directs a question to another student. She calls their attention to how Hutchinson gets the students up out of their seats and into small-group conversations with each other about issues of race and racism and encourages the students to recognize each other's turn to talk in the whole-class discussion. Ladson-Billings, like Grossman, also then asks her students to try out some of the strategies they identify in Hutchinson's class in their practicum field sites, videotape their teaching, and add it to their digital portfolios.

But there are some content area differences in how Ladson-Billings uses Hutchinson's site within the discipline of social studies. A focus of her course is for students to articulate how social studies teachers "help kids learn to be citizens in a democratic society" (Ladson-Billings, personal communication, February 25, 2008) and toward that end she invites her students to put together a "text-set" of developmentally appropriate literature on a social issue. Teaching about power and inequity, as Ladson-Billings observes, is "tricky, because the students themselves don't feel all that comfortable" discussing race and racism with children. By interrogating the ways in which Hutchinson frames her students' discussion of the "n-word" in the Ruff text and in their everyday discourse, Ladson-Billings's students can think about how to facilitate class conversations on controversial topics, on not only race and racism, but also poverty, homelessness, immigration, political change, civic engagement, and so on. Additionally, the mutual use of each other's work by Hutchinson and Ladson-Billings reinforces a significant outcome of "going public" with K–12 practice: subverting the traditional power dynamic between university-based research expertise and school-based wisdom of practice. Instead of engaging in a top-down university-school relationship, Ladson-Billings and Hutchinson become colleagues in conversation about issues of mutual concern.

Foundational Connection: Anna Richert

Anna Richert is a professor of education at Mills College. In her course on adolescent development, she uses Hutchinson's work along with several others as "silent teaching partners" as described on her MRT "Learning About Adolescents from Teachers Who Teach Them Well" (Richert, 2006). Richert observed that her secondary teaching students often came to their studies with a considerable love for their subject area but only a peripheral sense of why they would need to know about adolescents as learners in a particular developmental stage. By integrating Hutchinson's work into her class, Richert can create a content connection for preservice English teachers, subsequently opening up for a whole-class conversation about how different teachers approach the challenges of curriculum and pedagogy in middle and high school contexts.

Richert considers there to be three central texts for her course: the "silent teaching partners" whose practices are documented on their websites, the course readings, and the voices of adolescent learners themselves. To bring together all three, Richert developed an innovative outreach project in which local high school students visit her class as "experts" in adolescent development (Viadero, 2005). As Richert describes on her website:

> We were joined for the day by a group of high school students whose teachers are two Mills grads. When the students arrived they were assigned Mills partners with whom they worked for the afternoon. The Mills students had selected something from one of the websites they had studied that they found puzzling about teaching or learning as it was portrayed on the site. The goal

was to share that puzzle with the high school student and discuss it to get the high schooler's perspective on the events that the clip portrayed. A more general conversation about teaching and learning in the high school setting followed. (2006)

There were significant outcomes for both sides of this exchange. The high school partners engaged confidently and animatedly in this exchange, comfortably slipping into their roles as "experts" in the conversation. One observed, "I think that every student should have to think about what teachers have to go through. . . . It was cool because we got to teach someone older than us, how to teach." Another commented that seeing how engaged the preservice teacher was by his expertise "made us want to learn, made us want to listen to him." Another student described how she would take the learnings from the day back to her own school setting: "It made me want to be a better student for the teachers because they go through so much work for us. It also opens our eyes, as students, to *how* we should learn, the different ways we can learn."

The Mills students were similarly transformed by the experience, especially by seeking expertise from the high school students about how best to serve them as learners. One remarked, "I was able to give the best of myself as a listener and create that connection with the child." Another noted, "So much of school is about teachers knowing and kids not knowing— teachers holding, therefore, power, and kids not. This project really allows for an opportunity for kids to hold knowledge too." These learnings are pivotal for those about to begin their teaching careers. Another of Anna's students observed that the collaborative project "puts you in a situation where you feel like you have a lot of power. You feel like you have a lot of weight on your shoulders. You're learning what you have to do, so it makes you want to go and do that even better."

By looking collaboratively at Hutchinson's practice (among others), the high school students and the teacher candidates were able to begin their conversation about a neutral common text; instead of beginning by either critiquing the other's experiences and practices as a teacher or learner, they were able to bring their individual perspectives to a record of others' school experiences and link their insights into agendas of change for each.

Hutchinson's Work in Other Environments of Teacher Learning

Grossman, Ladson-Billings, and Richert are just three examples of how Hutchinson's practice connects to different environments of preservice teacher education. Hutchinson herself makes regular reference to the site in her work with novice and veteran teaching colleagues in the Los Angeles area. Lee Shulman, president emeritus of the Carnegie Foundation, commented, "We are using our analyses of Hutchinson's teaching to develop more powerful theoretical principles for teaching and learning literacy, especially in creating bridges between the interpretations of text and the active use of discussion and dialogue among students" (2005). Still other applications have yet to be invented, but all rest on a careful reading of Yvonne's classroom and a creative vision of how her practice can extend other educators' professional learning. Your insights and innovations are now part of that progression!

QUESTIONS FOR REFLECTION AND CONVERSATION

- How might you use aspects of Yvonne Hutchinson's practice for teacher learning in your context?
- What would be the key elements of an anatomy of your classroom?
- How would you place these elements in an explicit structure framing your practice?
- What artifacts would elaborate audiences' understanding of these events of practice, your students' work, your teaching context, major influences on your work, and your professional history?

Jennifer Myers:
Chronicling a Classroom
Literacy Environment

J ENNIFER MYERS teaches second grade in Morgan Hill, California, a community of about 35,000 located 25 miles south of San Jose. Her students at Barrett Elementary live in homes where Spanish or English (or both) are spoken; their parents work in Silicon Valley dot-com ventures and on Central Valley fruit farms. I came to know Jennifer through one of her former education professors, Katharine Samway of San Jose State University. Samway told me that she took her teacher preparation students to Myers's class to observe and had had Myers come to her class to do demonstration lessons on reading and writing workshop. The workshop approach to the teaching of literacy is something that many teachers, schools, and districts are eager to try out, but with few examples of how to do it well. We suspected that educational audiences might respond to an image of how these practices are enacted in one classroom.

When I first spoke with Myers, she was surprised by the invitation to make her teaching practice public, because she was only at the end of her 4th year of teaching. I emphasized to her, however, that many novice teachers might feel that the practices of a "near peer" would be more accessible and relevant to their own professional development. Myers herself had initially developed her workshop approach through a professional development partnership between her school district and the Noyce Foundation's Every Child a Reader and Writer program. (See Chapter 7 for more about how the ECRW program made its work with teachers public.) Her school faculty also participated in faculty "book clubs" around professional and pedagogical issues and had read Lucy McCormick Calkins's *The Art of Teaching Reading* (2001). Myers's professional practice already encompassed reflections about how she might integrate those approaches into her literacy block instruction.

Having robust images of particularly effective practices in a high-stakes curricular area like early elementary language arts is of special importance, as teachers and schools try to rapidly address student achievement gaps in response to state and federal expectations for literacy. Myers agreed that she was eager to share her own practices, but emphasized that she was continuing to develop and refine her literacy instruction; she did not want to have any representation of her teaching be presented as "best practices." She spoke warmly of how rewarding it was to invite Samway's education students into her classroom and to contribute to her future colleagues' consideration of how they might begin to view students as writers. Making a public record of her practice would allow Myers to elaborate these conversations with vivid exemplars of her work with her students.

GOING PUBLIC WITH MYERS'S CLASS: THE LITERACY WORKSHOP APPROACH

In her professional development experiences as well as in her reflective conversations with her teaching colleagues, Myers was in an active state of developing and refining her practices in literacy instruction. We spoke about what parts of her practice she might want to share, and she described that the "rituals and routines" informing her literacy instruction were present nearly every morning during their 2 hours of literacy workshop.

When we first spoke it was May 2004; the end of the school year was fast approaching. However, by inviting Myers to be explicit about these rituals and routines that support her literacy instruction throughout the year, we suspected that we might be able to give audiences a sense of that longitudinal development of students' literacy competence. We also thought that because Myers herself was so explicit about the influences shaping her literacy instruction, we would include a section of her record of practice in which she detailed them for interested audiences.

CONTENT FOCUS: THE READING AND WRITING WORKSHOP APPROACH

Every morning, Myers spent the first 2½ hours of her classroom day in reading and writing workshop. She explained, "I really make it a point to keep the schedule the same each day in my room for consistency. I find that the kids do very well with the predictable schedule on a regular basis." That schedule included the following:

8:00–8:15   Readers' workshop: Short read-aloud with a mini-lesson

8:15–8:25	Independent reading: Teacher confers with students one on one (I do not get to all of my students in one day, but will confer with all sometime during the week)
8:25–9:10	Independent reading with independent work: Teacher meets with three different guided reading groups (first group from 8:25 to 8:40, second group from 8:40 to 8:55, third group from 8:55 to 9:10)
9:10–9:15	Share with the whole class
9:15–9:35	Recess
9:35–10:00	Word study (focus on grammar, frequently used words, punctuation, and word groups)
10:00–10:15	Writers workshop: Minilesson
10:15–10:50	Independent writing with one-on-one teacher conferring
10:50–11:00	Share with whole class
11:00–11:45	Lunch

On that morning, Myers was focusing her reading workshop on "text-to-text" connections, and her writing workshop on expanding jottings from a notebook into the beginnings of an original story.

PRACTITIONER GOALS

At the beginning of the year, Myers's emphasis on the establishment of "rituals and routines" supported her students' literacy development throughout the year. During those first few months, she did explicit teaching around these rituals and routines, on topics such as selecting a "just right book," how to show active listening, and the role of a draft in the writing process, to name only a few. As Myers explained to me, her goals at the end of the year built on these foundational literacy approaches from the beginning of the year, and she planned to do some reteaching of major concepts the students had learned during the course of the year:

> Here, we were talking about text-to-text connections, which is a comprehension tool. I modeled for them with my read-out-loud how to do a text-to-text connection, and then I told them, when you go back and do your independent reading today, if you have a text-to-text connection, I want you to take a sticky note, note the page, and continue reading.

During writing workshop, Myers wanted her students to examine their story ideas and consider which of them they might begin to expand into a story. To accomplish this, she modeled her own process as a writer.

During the writers workshop minilesson, I am modeling what I would like the students to try by using my own personal notebook. I think it is important for the students to see that I am a writer as well in the classroom. Since this was at the end of the school year, I am having my students revisit their previous notebook entries in the hopes that maybe they will want to turn an old entry into a new one. The notebooks in my classroom are not a journal, but rather a place for students to collect their ideas for future stories.

Both of these focus on the importance of identifying components of text and either expanding them or connecting them to other texts. Myers wanted her students to live the lives of readers and writers by internalizing this active engagement with text.

DOCUMENTATION OF THE LITERACY WORKSHOP

Jennifer Myers followed the same structure for her literacy instruction every day. Before the students entered the classroom that June morning, I walked slowly around the perimeter of her carpeted classroom as soft classical music played on a small CD player in the corner of the room. Like my own elementary classroom, Myers's instructional space was a visual record of where they'd been in the months before, and I used the videocamera on "photo" setting to take stills of the walls, in their entirety as well as in closeup. The walls of Myers's room were divided into sections focusing on areas of the curriculum; a significant proportion of the wall space in the corner opposite the door was devoted to reading and writing workshop. In this 12' × 12' open corner space, Myers had placed a welcoming rocking chair adjacent to an easel in front of a brightly colored carpet with a grid design. On the walls of this corner, Myers had placed handmade posters and documents relevant to students' literacy and calling back to the establishment of the class rituals and routines, with titles such as

- What Is a Just Right Book?
- What Good Readers Do
- When Readers *Infer*, They:
- Author's Chair Guidelines
- Partner Share
- Capital Letters Guidelines
- Instead of "Said," Use:
- What You Can Do When You've Finished Writing
- Getting Help During Writers Workshop

Myers's students made reference to these contextual supports during the independent work components of her reading and writing workshop sessions. Both of her workshop blocks were structured similarly: There was an opening lesson of approximately 10 minutes, a period of independent work during which Myers conferenced with students, and a closure/celebration period in which students shared their reading and writing work with the larger group.

Opening of Class

The opening bell rang and Myers's students lined up outside her classroom. As they entered, they greeted her with "Good morning, Mrs. Myers," hung up their jackets and backpacks on hooks by the door, and walked to the open corner. Myers said, "Good morning, boys and girls," and thanked them for sitting "crisscross applesauce." I stood next to the group with my handheld video camera braced against the side of my body, monitor facing up so that I could see what I was recording.

Reading Workshop

After Myers had taken attendance and counted the numbers of students wanting a hot lunch for the day, she introduced the day's focus: making explicit connections between a book they're reading and others they'd read before.

Reading workshop minilesson. Her readaloud selection corresponded to her "teaching point"; that day, she had selected Strega Nona by Tomie DePaola (1975, 1993), a familiar and prolific children's author.

> MYERS: Boys and girls, today in readers workshop we are going to begin another Tomie DePaola story. This one we've heard before, but we know that good readers go back and we reread. This one is called *Strega Nona*. Part of the reason why I'm reading you another Tomie DePaola book today is because we are going to be making text-to-text connections again. Who can raise their hand and tell me what a text-to-text connection is? Drea.
>
> DREA: A text-to-text connection is like when you connect it to another book.
>
> MYERS: Yeah. Something in one book reminds you of something that happened in another book. And I have a feeling that today we're going to be making a lot of text-to-text connections to *Strega Nona*. So let's get started reading this book, and

as I read it out loud, I want you to be noticing any text-to-text connections you have.

As she animatedly read the text to the students, Myers occasionally stopped to invite the children to contribute their observations about similarities between *Strega Nona* and other books with their "shoulder partners":

> FELIPE: I have a text-to-text connection. In the book *Strega Nona Meets Her Match*, it's by the same author.
>
> GRANT: Oh. Well, I noticed that—it's sort of a noticing and a text-to-text connection too. I noticed, I'm connecting the book *Strega Nona* to *Strega Nona Meets Her Match*, the same book that you said. Um, because again, Strega Nona went to meet Strega Amelia.

After she completed reading the book to the students, Myers dismissed them to their desks for independent reading. The students went to their cubbies, extracted their books, and sat at their desks.

Independent reading work: Conferencing. Myers waited for all the children to be seated, then drew a chair up next to one student at his desk. She described that she uses the same approach with all her reader conferences, opening and closing the interactions with nearly the same script:

> Readers conferences are important during independent reading time for many reasons. For one, it allows me to differentiate instruction for all of my learners. I can find a teaching point for each student, and teach to it. In addition, it allows me to check to see if the independent reading book the student has selected is a just right book for them. When I conduct a readers conference, I always begin by pointing out one thing I noticed the reader is doing that is positive. Then, as I listen to them read, I find the teaching point that I would like to leave the student with. During this time, it is also important to take an informal running record. This can be used for assessment purposes later on.
>
> Students in readers workshop read all different-level books; however, the same strategies are taught to each reader in the classroom. Most of the time, I will ask students to use one of their strategies to help them when they are stuck on a word or phrase. These strategies should be modeled thoroughly by the teacher before expecting the students to reference them on their own. An example that I teach my students is to "sound out the word" if they are stuck on the word. I always make the student repeat back to

me what they will plan on working on. Then, I use that time to write down the teaching point in my conference notes.

Readers conference 1: *Grant.* In her readers workshop conference with her student Grant, Myers illustrates this approach. During the conference, she made brief notes about her "teaching points" on a classroom grid chart on a clipboard. In their interaction, Grant surprised Myers by making reference to one of the posters in the reading workshop wall.

MYERS: Hi, Grant.
GRANT: Hi, Ms. Myers.
MYERS: What are you reading today?
GRANT: I'm working on *Magic Treehouse: Ghost Town at Sundown.*
MYERS: And do you know what your job is today during readers workshop?
GRANT: Text-to-text connections.
MYERS: Okay. So when you find a text-to-text connection, what do I want you to do?
GRANT: Put a sticky note on the page where it is.
MYERS: Perfect. Can I hear you read out loud to me?

Grant began to read a section of the book in which the lead characters, Jack and Annie, encounter an "enchantress librarian." She held up her hand, and Grant stopped reading aloud.

MYERS: I'm going to stop you for a moment. *Enchantress.* Do you know what that word means?
GRANT: Like, sort of enchanted, like it's, um . . .
MYERS: What does *enchanted* mean?
GRANT: Sort of like a magic spell or something?
MYERS: Mmm hmm. And what clues told you what that word meant when you read it? How did you know the meaning of that word? What helped you?
GRANT: The word *enchanted* just helped me some.
MYERS: So you knew what the word *enchanted* was, and so that helped.
GRANT: And *enchantress* is like, um, um, ah . . . A female, female magician, I think?
MYERS: So when you're reading, and when you come across words that you're not really sure what the meaning is, what do you do to help yourself as a reader? You stop and you . . .
GRANT: . . . infer?
MYERS: Yeah! You can make, you can *infer*, definitely!

Myers then invited Grant to continue reading on and, after another paragraph, asked him to summarize the content of the text he'd just read and any predictions he held for the text. As she closed the reading conference, she reinforced what he was doing as a reader, leaving him with something to work on:

> MYERS: Grant, one thing that I want to compliment you on, is that as you're reading, you're doing an excellent job of reading all of the punctuation. For example, when you see quotation marks, you're really reading like the person is actually talking. . . . You're reading with a lot of expression. That's really smart. One thing that I want you to work on while you're doing your independent reading is making sure that you're keeping track of what's going on in the story.
>
> GRANT: That I understand what's happening?
>
> MYERS: Exactly. And if something doesn't make sense to do you, while you're reading, stop and reread, and that should help you understand what's going on. Okay? Good job, Grant.

In this interaction, Grant demonstrates that he not only had a developed sense of his task for the day as a reader, but also drew upon the environmental supports for his reading. He made explicit reference to the idea that good readers "infer." Not 10 feet from his desk, Grant could easily see Myers's poster on inference (Figure 5.1). Myers left Grant at the end of the reading conference with a reinforcement of the things that came easily

Figure 5.1. Screen shot of Jennifer Myers's "When Readers Infer" poster.

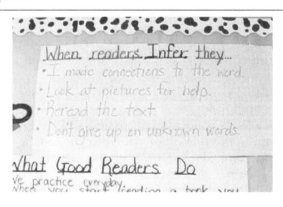

to him as a reader as well as the things he was working to develop. Although her conversations in the four other readers conferences that day were on different books and resulted in different teaching points, Myers similarly reinforced each child's strengths and pointed out their areas of improvement in a positive, constructive manner.

After the first 15 minutes of independent reading time, Myers rang a small bell to attract the students' attention and reminded them to write down the text-to-text connections they found in preparation for sharing in the large group during closure.

Independent Reading Work: Guided Reading Group

After this reminder, Myers called a group of students to a small semicircular table and led them through a guided reading group process (see Fountas & Pinnell, 1996). Like reading conferences, guided reading allowed Myers to focus on individual student differences in reading comprehension, do some direct teaching, and conduct detailed running records (Clay, 1993) of children's reading capabilities.

> My guided reading groups always follow the same structure and time frame—they typically last 15 minutes each. The structure is as follows: Students reread a familiar book while I take a running record for assessment, a new book is introduced by me with vocabulary development, students practice reading it on their own, and while I listen to them read I leave each student with a teaching point. Then the whole group comes back together to discuss a strategy or skill I think they would all benefit on working on. Guided reading is important because it allows for differentiation in the classroom. Through guided reading, I am able to meet the levels of all of my readers.

That day, Myers's students reread *The Flood* (Giles, 1994) while she did a running record of the same book for one student. Then, she introduced the new book, *The Toy Farm* (Giles, 1997):

> MYERS: Today, I'm really excited. Because today, we're going to begin a brand-new book. Let me go ahead and tell you about the book. The name of this book is called *The Toy Farm*. Let me take my sticky notes off of it so you can see. *The Toy Farm*. Now, if you're going to make a prediction about what *The Toy Farm* is going to be about, what do you predict? Jasmine?
>
> JASMINE: I think that it's going to be about, there's a bunch of toys,

> like that, and it's like a real farm, and playing with the farm,
> like if it was a real farm?
>
> MYERS: Okay, so you're thinking that maybe this farm is make-
> believe?
>
> JASMINE: Yes.
>
> MYERS: That it's not real. Okay, very good. Who has a different
> prediction? Who has a prediction that's a little bit different
> from Jasmine's? Tell me, then, what do you notice that's
> happening on the cover? Annette, what's something you
> notice that's happening on the cover?
>
> ANNETTE: There's animals?
>
> MYERS: There's animals. Do you think those animals are real?
>
> ANNETTE: No.

Myers continued asking her six guided-reading group members to make predictions about the text based on the cover, and then turned to reading the text, connecting the structure of this story—problem and solution—to ideas she later emphasized during writing workshop.

> MYERS: Today, you're going to read about the toy farm. And in this
> story there's a big problem. But also in the story, there's a
> solution. What's a solution, again? What does *solution* mean?
>
> ANNETTE: When they solve the problem.
>
> MYERS: Right, how the problem was solved.

Myers distributed individual copies of *The Toy Farm* to each student and then listened to each of the six read aloud while the other students read silently. For each student, Myers left each interaction with a teaching point reminding her or him of the challenges identified in their reading and had the student repeat back to her "what you're going to work on today in your reading." The consistency of her approach supported her students as they responded by clearly restating her teaching points. Not a single student answered with a lowered head, shrug, or "I don't know."

Reading Workshop Closure: Sharing Text-to-Text Connections

The final 10 minutes of Myers's reading workshop hour was spent in whole-group sharing. The students came back to the carpeted area, this time arranging themselves in a circle, and shared the text-to-text connections they had identified. Some compared their books to others by the same author; others identified similar artistic choices. Most made point-to-point direct comparisons: "Both books have a cat," or "In the book *Tea at the TreeDome*, Spongebob smelled something nasty, and in the book *The Berenstain Bears*, the mom and dad smell something nasty." Others identified larger comparative themes: "In the book *Stuart Little* . . . he's different from his family, and in *Trumpet of the Swan* he's different from his family." The students were eager to hear each other's observations about their books, some exclaiming excitedly when they realized that they shared a text-to-text connection with another student in the class.

WORD STUDY

After the conclusion of Myers's reading workshop, she engaged them in a brief "word study" intended to develop their accuracy in spelling. As she explained:

> Word study is taught separately from writers workshop. I spend 20 minutes daily on teaching word study. The dry erase whiteboards have been a useful tool that I use to help teach various skills. They are easy to clean, with zero prep work involved. I always make sure that I teach my students how to correctly use the whiteboards, dry erase pens, and erasers. Word study encompasses many different things. Some things that are taught during word study time include high-frequency words, grammar, and punctuation.

The students wrote their responses to given words on individual white boards, turning them around to show Myers the answers. After three "high-frequency" words (*could, been*, and *make*) and two new sound-alike word groups (*which/witch* and *their/there/they're*), Myers adjourned her literacy block instruction and dismissed the students who were "sitting quietly in their table groups" to recess.

WRITING WORKSHOP

After their midmorning recess, Myers again began on the carpet, opening her minilesson with a description of the day's focus. This excerpt shows how Myers moved from reminding students what they'd done before, telling them the day's focus, modeling expected writing behaviors, facilitating brainstorming, and dismissing students to their independent work in writing workshop.

Myers: Good morning, writers!

Class: Good morning, Mrs. Myers!

Myers: So! Not yesterday but the day before, we went on a noticings walk. And we went outside, and we went and we noticed all of the things that were happening around us. As writers, I wanted you to go and make a list using dash-facts of all of the things you were seeing around you. Then I told you that you were going to have to go and look back at that list, because you could take one of those ideas and form it into a story, or possibly a notebook entry.

Writing Workshop Minilesson

Myers began by modeling this process in her own writing, moving from her own noticings to select one that she might want to expand into the beginnings of an original story.

Today I would like to share with you the noticings that I wrote down from—these are actually older noticings. These are things that I wrote at the beginning of the year when we went on our first noticings walk. I'm going to reread it to myself right now, and as I'm rereading it, I'm going to ask myself, "Hmm. Are there any of these noticings I could make into a notebook entry later on?" So here's what I wrote. I'm going to wait for everyone's attention. "Miss Stuart has yard duty." I don't know if I could really make that into a story. So I'm going to keep on reading on. "A boy is kicking a ball *after* the bell rings." That's an interesting noticing, but you know what? I don't really think I could make that into a notebook entry or a story. So I'm going to keep reading on. "Cars are whizzing by on the freeway. The noise is bothering me!" That might make an interesting story. . . . I could talk about driving on the freeway . . . but I'm going to keep reading on. "A first grader is running through the hall." Mmm, that might make an interesting story about school rules, but I think I have a better one here. "Today is a really hot day, but we are in the shade, so it's cooler." Ah . . . you know what? That's actually bringing me back to the memory of the day that all of us at the start of the year went out to do our first noticings tour. So you know what I think I'm going to do? I'm going to write a notebook entry on that noticing.

Having reminded the students of their prior work, Myers then directly modeled the writing task she expected them to engage in that day.

Here's what I did. As a writer, I went and I took my pen, and I circled my noticing in blue. You're going to be circling your noticing today that you selected in crayon. That way it really stands out to you. Now what I'm going to do is I'm going to reread my noticing and think of a story that I can write from it. The one that I selected for today says, "Today is a really hot day, but we are in the shade, so it's cooler." And now I'm ready to start to write a story.

I started working on this a little bit this morning, because I wanted to get a head start. Here's what I wrote so far. "I can still remember the day when I took my second graders out for a walk to do some writers workshop noticings. It was one of the hottest days of the year! I decided to move my students to the shade near the ball wall so they wouldn't get too hot." Okay? And I stopped there because I'm going to continue thinking about how I'm going to write this story. Okay? Right now, I want you to share with your shoulder partner a possible noticing you wrote about that you might want to select to write more on today.

Myers's students turned to each other on the carpet and animatedly shared their ideas in groups of twos and threes.

> DIANA (to her partner): I could write about seeing the moon up in the sky . . .
> GRANT (to his partner): You know what, Felipe? I think that that would make a very good notebook entry.

Myers then summarized what she heard in the pair-share conversations and prepared the students for their independent writing work.

> MYERS: Okay. Come back to me in 5, 4, 3, 2; thank you. Now. What I wanted you to do today is I wanted you to go back into your notebook and reread the noticings that you wrote down the other day from our walk. Aaron had a really good question. He said, "I was absent that day. What should I do?" You can go back to the first one we did, *way* back in September, and reread those. Then, I wanted you to go and select one noticing you had so you can write more about that today in your notebook. Who would like to share one of the noticings that they wrote down the other day that they're going to make into a story in their notebook today? All right. Kenny!
> KENNY: The spider one.

MYERS: Okay, tell me about the spider one. What did you write about the spider? What did you notice about the spider?

KENNY: That it was on David's notebook.

MYERS: Okay. So you're thinking about writing a story about the spider that was on David's notebook. That sounds like a really interesting story! David, I think that sounds like a great story for him to write about. Maybe he can even get some ideas from . . .

DAVID: I don't like it when people look at me.

MYERS: I know, that can be embarrassing sometimes. But you know what? I don't think they mean it in a negative way. I think they're just saying, "That's pretty cool!" Kenny's going to write about you! That's neat! Who has a different one, a different noticing than Kenny's? Okay? Felicia.

FELICIA: I was going to write about the empty playground.

MYERS: What about the empty playground? What are you thinking about writing about in your story?

FELICIA: A fiction book about when kids don't have to have any recess.

MYERS: Oh, you're going to write a fiction story about how kids don't have any recess. That sounds interesting. Okay. Rest your arms. Today, when you go back to your seat, Kenny, I want you to go and reread the noticings that you wrote the other day. Then I want you in crayon to circle one that you think you're going to be able to write more about. Then, when you've selected that, you're going to turn to a blank page inside your notebook, and start writing your story. Okay? If you finish writing early, then you need to go and read the poster here that says what you can do if you're finished writing. I'll be coming around and conferencing with each of you. Does anyone have a question about what your job is today in writers workshop? Jasmine.

JASMINE: Are we gonna be, like, in the author's chair?

MYERS: I will be selecting some students today for the Author's Chair. Okay? All right. . . . If you know what your job is today as a writer, you may quietly go back to your seat.

Myers turned on some quiet classical music and began circulating around for writing conferences.

Independent Writing Work: Conferencing

Myers used a similar script for the opening and closing of her writing conferences: "Tell me what you're working on today as a writer" and "Tell

me what you're going to work on now as a writer." Because the level
of expressiveness was high—students could elaborate any one of their
"noticings" in their notebook to begin developing into a story—the conferences themselves followed the students' own craft choices.

Writing conference 1: Douglas. In her first conference, Douglas shared that
he couldn't decide between two of his noticing fragments: "There's a mi-
rage on the house" and "I have a headache." His noticings mirrored those
modeled by Myers in her minilesson, focusing on the heat of the day. In
conversation with him, Myers refrained from telling him which of the two
she thought was more compelling, instead encouraging the student to reflect on which of his story options *he* preferred.

> Myers: Hi, Douglas.
> Douglas: Hi.
> Myers: So tell me what you're working on today as a writer.
> Douglas: I'm working on trying to choose a noticing that I could,
> that would be useable to turn it . . .
> Myers: Into a possible story?
> Douglas: Yeah.
> Myers: Or even a noticing that you know you can write more
> about, huh.
> Douglas: Yeah.
> Myers: Okay! So do you have some in mind. . . . Let me move this
> over here so I can see. Do you have any in mind at this time?
> Douglas: I have about two . . .
> Myers: That you're thinking of?
> Douglas: But I don't know much about either of them.
> Myers: That's all right! Can you share with me the two that you're
> thinking of?
> Douglas: "I have a headache" and also "There's a mirage on the house."
> Myers: There's a mirage on the house . . .
> Douglas: Yeah, it looked like it.
> Myers: Let me ask you this: What one do you think you can write
> more about right now, or, appeals to you more? You selected
> "There's a mirage on the house" and "I have a headache."
> What one do you think you can write a lot more about?
> Douglas: Well, probably, I think that I can write about headaches,
> because . . .
> Myers: Headaches. I'm wondering why you had a headache that day!
> Douglas: It was getting very hot, and it felt like a lot of pressure.

MYERS: So you might be writing, then, on a memory of when you were starting to feel not so well in the middle of writers workshop.

DOUGLAS: Or I could write a nonfiction piece about how headaches are caused?

MYERS: Okay! So you're just . . . you're not really sure about what type of story you want to write. I'm here today in this conference to help you decide what one you're going to write more on in your notebook. So. Do you feel comfortable making that decision, that you want to write more about the headache? So what do you need to do, once you've selected it, what do you need to do?

DOUGLAS: I have to circle it with the crayon . . .

MYERS: Exactly.

DOUGLAS: And I have to see if I can make it into an entry.

MYERS: Okay! Great! So now that you have your idea, you can try to write more about that. It looks like you've turned to a blank page. I'd like you to put the date at the top, and I'm going to let you get started on writing more about this topic, okay? Right now, we don't know if it's going to be fiction or nonfiction. You can just expand more on the noticing that you had the other day and see if you can build from that. Okay?

DOUGLAS: Yeah, that sounds good.

MYERS: Do you feel comfortable with that topic?

(Douglas nods.)

MYERS: Okay. So tell me what you're going to do today in writers workshop.

DOUGLAS: I'm going to try making this idea into a notebook entry which would be about either my headache or headaches.

MYERS: Okay, sounds good! Sounds like a plan. I'm going to let you get to work, okay? All right. Good job, Douglas.

Writing conference 2: Vanessa. A subsequent student conference shows a student, Vanessa, in a different place with her writing: having selected a noticing, she was already started on developing and expanding it into a story. Interestingly, Vanessa's idea echoes the noticing Kenny shared in the whole group minilesson. But just as in the conference with Douglas, Myers's interaction with Vanessa encouraged the student to stretch beyond where she was working independently, to focus on a teaching point, and to share her story during that day's "Author's Chair" at the end of the writing workshop.

MYERS: Vanessa, tell me what you're working on today as a writer.

VANESSA: I'm writing a true and fake story about how the spider attacked David's notebook.

MYERS: So let's go back to what you decided for your . . .

(Vanessa slides a loose piece of paper to Myers.)

MYERS: Oh! That's right, you didn't have your notebook that day. You selected "bags on notebooks."

VANESSA: Bugs.

MYERS: Oh, bugs. I'm sorry. Bugs on notebooks. So you also saw all those bugs that were crawling on his notebook. You must have been sitting really close to him. All right! So would you like to read so far what you've done here?

VANESSA: "I think it was a few days ago. Yes! It was terrifying! A spider, yes, a spider on David's notebook! A innocent bug was killed. Yes, it was killed. The killed, innocent bug. The notebook won the battle. David's notebook was the one and only champion. The end."

MYERS: That sounds like a really funny, catchy story. And you wanted to write it, kind of like a fiction story, but it really did happen to David, but kind of built off of that, huh? Wow. That sounds like you have done a really lot of making . . . taking your noticing and expanding on it, and making it into a much bigger piece. That's really smart, Vanessa. So what are your plans now in writers workshop today?

VANESSA: To look at the poster of what you have to do after you're done.

MYERS: You know, you can do that, or I have another idea for you. You did such a great job of taking your noticing and expanding on it, maybe you might want to take another noticing and write more about that. Because, you know, one day, you can take one of these notebook entries and publish it in writers workshop when we start to publish again. I think that a better plan for now would be to look at your list and see if you can take any of those ideas and make another notebook entry on it. What do you think about that?

VANESSA: Yeah. I can try that.

MYERS: All right. Now, I have a question for you. Would you like to share this piece today in the Author's Chair?

VANESSA: Yeah.

MYERS: Okay. I'd love to have you do that. So tell me, now that you're finished with this, what are you going to work on now as a writer?

VANESSA: I'm going to try to find another one of these and make it
　　　into a story.
MYERS: Excellent job. I'll let you get started.

Myers explained to me that her Author's Chair sharing rotates among the
students, so they all have an opportunity to share their writing formally
in front of the whole class.

Writing Workshop: Author's Chair

After 40 minutes of writing conferences and student independent work,
Myers rang a quiet bell and the class fell silent. She invited them again
back to the carpet, and Vanessa made her way to the brown rocking chair
previously occupied by Myers during the minilesson. As Vanessa shared
her story, she giggled as she animatedly told the story of "Bug vs. Notebook." Even David, who had expressed his discomfort with everyone
"looking at me," laughed and sat up a little straighter during Vanessa's
storytelling. After she'd finished reading, Myers invited the students to
contribute their responses and suggestions to Vanessa as a writer. David
and Kenny were the first to chime in.

MYERS: So you did a very good job. . . . Check yourselves, boys and
　　　girls; thank you. You did a great job of making it into a
　　　humorous story. Now Vanessa, part of the reason I had you
　　　do this is because, one day, if I were to ask you to publish
　　　maybe a memory, you could write about the memory you
　　　had of when you saw bugs crawling over it. You could take
　　　some of those lines from your notebook and use it when
　　　you're drafting. Okay? So that is a smart start to your story.
　　　Great job! Can someone raise their hand and give Vanessa a
　　　positive comment?
VANESSA: David.
DAVID: I think that was a funny book.
MYERS: Okay, and why? You need to be able to say why.
DAVID: Because, um, you made us laugh, because you were talking
　　　about who won the battle of spider vs. notebook.
MYERS: A humorous notebook entry. Very good. Does anyone
　　　have an appropriate suggestion for Vanessa, or something that
　　　you would like her to try next time?
KENNY: I like how you said, um, the book won the battle, but
　　　wouldn't you say what happened to the spider? Like, did he
　　　get squished or something? You could add that in.

MYERS: So it sounds like, Vanessa, Kenny wanted more details
     about how the spider was squished. Would you feel like that
     would be appropriate for your story?
VANESSA: Yeah. I'll add that.
MYERS: Okay. Let's give Vanessa a big silent applause.
(All the students wave their hands and fingers in the air.)
MYERS: Excellent job. Thank you, Vanessa.

After the second student shared her work in Author's Chair, Myers com-
mended the students on their excellent work and dismissed them by table
groups to line up at the classroom door for lunch and recess.

REFLECTION ON THE DAY

After her students left the classroom, Myers and I sat down and talked about
the morning's instruction. She spoke about how the workshop approach
contributed to her literacy instruction and her students' development:

> In the readers workshop and the writers workshop, the great thing
> about it is that you have that individual conference time. So the
> kids, for example, in readers workshop, they're all reading books at
> their level, or pretty close to it. Sometimes they select books out of
> the library that are way off base and we have to redirect them, but
> the great thing is that I can have these one-on-one conferences
> with them and give them their strategies that they specifically need
> help with, place it in their mind, "Okay, today I'm teaching you
> this." I always try to give them something positive that they're
> doing, and then I try to leave them with a teaching point, like,
> "You're doing a really good job reading with expression when you
> have the quotation marks there. However, you're still forgetting
> that. . . . You're not reading the word through." I try to leave them
> with a teaching point and then I record it on my conference notes,
> so they're being held accountable and I'm being held accountable,
> and I can chart their progress and assess them.

Myers also described the importance of the foundations provided by her
"rituals and routines" set in the beginning of the school year:

> In the 1st month or 6–8 weeks of school, you are just drilling them
> with the rituals and routines of readers workshop and writers
> workshop, constant practice and reinforcement every day. We're in

June now; that's why they've been so successful. Me, as a teacher, being consistent every single day. My structure has not changed at all. Every day, they know we're going to do readers workshop, then we're going to recess, then we're going to word study, then we're doing writers workshop. By keeping that structure and the schedule real tight, by me being consistent and basically laying the foundation down for them those first 6–8 weeks, I really think that that has enabled me to become successful with them this year. People say, "Oh, my gosh! Six to 8 weeks of rituals and routines!" But it will make your life so much easier when you're in November and you're going, you know what? They know how to come to the carpet quietly. They know how to get a whiteboard. They know I'm going to call this group. They know to wait at their table until I call their table number. Constantly practicing that, putting in that time at the beginning of the year, I don't regret doing it at all. It really helps.

We discussed that the website would advance these ideas by emphasizing the workshop approach, the establishment of Myers's rituals and routines, and how she selects particular pieces of literature to support both efforts.

CREATING A MULTIMEDIA REPRESENTATION OF MYERS'S TEACHING

Once I'd returned to the Carnegie Foundation, I digitized Myers's videos using iMovie and spliced them into individual clips showing each event in order during the morning's instruction, from the opening routine, to readers workshop (minilesson, independent work and conferences, guided reading, and whole-group sharing), to word study, to writers workshop (minilesson, independent work and conferences, and Author's Chair whole-group sharing).

Artifacts from teachers' practice must be accompanied by teachers' commentary. Teachers are in the best position to identify subtleties about particular teaching events, explain mitigating factors, and call attention to students' subtle triumphs. We arranged for a substitute for Myers's class one day and she came to the Carnegie Foundation to reexamine each video clip and provide descriptive commentary for each. I inserted screenshots of each video into a Microsoft Word table, so that Myers could easily compose her commentary.

Myers especially wanted her MRT (Figure 5.2) to call attention to some of the features of her classroom teaching that are common to all teachers.

Figure 5.2. Screen shot of Jennifer Myers's MRT.

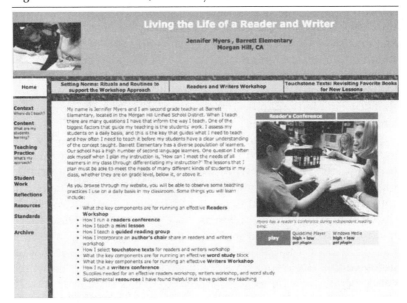

We made sure to integrate her descriptions of her content, her context, her teaching approach, the resources that inform and influence her practice, direct links to all student work samples gathered, and an "archive" containing all the artifacts gathered in her classroom. Along the left-hand side of the HTML site, we inserted a navigation bar with buttons for each of these sections. We also wanted to reinforce that each teacher is an individual and each classroom is a unique combination of people and practices. So along the top of Myers's website, we created three sections describing key emphases of Myers's approach:

- Setting Norms: Rituals and Routines to Support the Workshop Approach
- Readers and Writers Workshop
- Touchstone Texts: Revisiting Favorite Books for New Lessons

The text on each of these sections was drawn from our reflective conversation on the artifacts gathered from documentation day. In some instances, Myers elaborated her initial reflections with written e-mail narratives, and she wrote a brief description and commentary for each video clip.

We agreed that having a visual record of the three-dimensional learning environment would be important for visitors to understand the many resources Myers's students had available to them during independent reading and writing time. I took all the images I'd captured of Myers's walls and created image maps linking the image of the whole wall with close-ups of the individual posters (Figure 5.3) so that audiences could "zoom in" on individual posters and literacy supports.

HOW MYERS'S PRACTICE CAN BE USED FOR TEACHER LEARNING AND DEVELOPMENT

Throughout the workshop approach, Myers used a consistent interaction structure with each of her students. For audiences of this work, particularly novices to the profession, Myers's practices are explicit, close to the surface, and easy to identify and try out in another classroom context. This level of explicitness of approach, response, and outcomes can be readily adopted by other practitioners, especially those in the beginning years of their careers and looking to decentralize their literacy instruction to become more student driven.

Connections to Teacher Education

Establishment of classroom norms. Kathy Schultz of the University of Pennsylvania has used four different websites, Myers's among them, in her

Figure 5.3. Screen shot of interactive images of the classroom walls.

elementary literacy course to illustrate how teachers create rituals and routines to support children's literacy:

> I used the websites in several different ways. Sometimes I would ask the students to select a website to study at home in order to look for a particular ritual or routine that would tie to a discussion, activity or assignment for the next class. At other times I might show a video clip from the website in order to prompt a discussion (Schultz, 2006.)

In one class discussion, for example, Schultz asks her students to look closely at Myers's walls and then to identify connections between the environmental supports for literacy and the reading and writing workshop events.

Adoption of particular practices. Linda Kroll of Mills College also teaches elementary literacy to preservice teacher candidates. She has found that her students encounter challenges learning to lead a guided reading group. Kroll has them examine Myers's guided reading video (Kroll, 2006), images of her guided reading table, and the running record taken during the session; her students are then able to "try on" guided reading with a more developed understanding of how one teacher approaches the task.

Knowing students as literacy learners. Lucinda Pease-Alvarez teaches various courses on adapting instruction to meet the needs of English language learning students. In her multimedia representation of practice, Pease-Alvarez (2006) describes how she invites her University of California, Santa Cruz, students to examine the reading and writing workshop conferences for evidence of the power balance in Myers's relationships with her students. Her assignment asks students to identify patterns of facilitation in Myers's conferences; evidence of children's understandings of reading, writing, and language; and how Myers uses what she knows about students' lives in and out of school to inform her interactions with them.

Connections to a Global Network of Literacy Teachers

Surprisingly, we began to receive feedback on Jennifer Myers's site even before it was linked to the public gallery for the Carnegie Foundation. At the top of her website, we'd included a link inviting audiences to "give feedback on this website!" though it was intended for the teacher educator partners above who had provided initial feedback on Myers's site development. But e-mails started pouring in. One teacher after another sent unsolicited responses talking about how much they had got out of watching Myers's website. The e-mails came in from around the world, largely from teachers who had entered the terms *writing workshop* and *videos* into a search engine. The response to Myers's work began to illuminate an invisible professional community: that of individual teachers worldwide who were hungry to improve their literacy teaching. One teacher e-mailed from Thailand, saying that she had

> stumbled across your website this afternoon while preparing for a teachers training on reading and writing workshops. I can't believe that you are such a new teacher! After only a few years you have really got it down! Bravo! . . . I am doing a teacher training when school starts. We have graduated from three teachers to five this coming year and as the fifth-grade teacher I am hoping to get everyone "on the same page" so that by time the kids get to me they have some basic skills. Until now it has been every man for himself as far as teaching methods and strategies. Not working, believe me! Sadly, I had a group of fifth graders this year who read second-grade level and can't write a sentence, let alone a paragraph or story. They had never really written stories, if you can believe it! Anyway, if you wouldn't mind, I would like to show your videos to my teachers during our training. They are wonderfully done and so easy to follow.

Another teacher described transforming her literacy practices using Myers's site for guidance:

> I am a third-grade teacher in Georgia. This year, I am breaking the norm in my grade level to implement the workshop model. I have been relentlessly searching for materials and guidance this summer. Your site is wonderful!! It has been so helpful to me and so I am sending links to all of my colleagues in hopes that they, too, will be inspired.

Yet another teacher wrote commending Myers for her bravery in going public with her practice:

> I think it is really brave of you to put yourself out there like this so that many of the rest of us can "peek" inside your classroom. One of the worst things about teaching is that they never give you enough time to observe in other classrooms *once* you become a

teacher. You get lots of time when you are a student teacher, but after you've taught for several years, that's when you know what to look for and what you need to reinvigorate your classroom.

Local teachers who have found her site have even e-mailed Myers asking if they could visit her classroom in person. Myers commented how struck she is by the lack of a sense of community faced by the teachers who contact her about her website:

> I can't believe that I'm hearing from people all over the world, really, and they really are yearning for this kind of teaching, this philosophy. In some ways, it makes me a little bit sad that they have to go so far, that they're just not getting that from their administrators, or, their colleagues. I feel very blessed in the sense that I have an awesome principal. Really, I wouldn't be who I am without her really setting the tone of the school. Then also having my second-grade team. . . . We're spending time reflecting together and planning quality lessons that make sense and meet the needs of all of our students. I think that it's just building community there among the teachers. And that's what was making me sad before, with these teachers contacting me—I'm so excited that they're contacting me, but at the same time, why aren't they getting that same kind of help in their own school, in their own site?

These teachers, and many others who were moved to respond to Myers's work, are part of an invisible community—one that doesn't even realize its own interconnection. These teachers across the country (and globe) who are interested in developing their teaching competence, in this case, of literacy workshop practice, have a great deal to gain if they all become reinvigorated by gathering around touchstone records of teaching practice. How might literacy teaching be revolutionized and strengthened if all these teachers contacting Myers went public with their own reading and writing practices?

QUESTIONS FOR REFLECTION AND CONVERSATION

- How do you currently approach the teaching of reading and writing in your classroom?
- What common structures, rituals, and routines might you make public?
- What historical account of teaching and learning do your classroom walls provide?

Irma Lyons: Putting Faces
on a Learning Community

THE PHRASE *learning community* is often intoned in conversations about teaching and learning as if people knew what they were talking about. Is any group of people a learning community? Or do they have to have a consensus that they all belong to some common entity, working toward mutual learning goals? Is any classroom a learning community? Any school? Can a neighborhood or a city be learning communities?

Irma Lyons is the principal of the Will Rogers Learning Community elementary school in Santa Monica, California. Despite its proximity to the Pacific Ocean and some of the country's wealthiest communities, Will Rogers is an economically and ethnically diverse school. The 2005–2006 School Accountability Report Card (SARC) states that 53% of the 600 students at Will Rogers are Latino, 32% are White, 12% are African American, and 2% are Asian; 61% of the student population are listed as "socioeconomically disadvantaged" (SMMUSD, 2006). Before becoming principal, Lyons worked for 12 years at the school as a fifth-grade teacher. During her years in the classroom, she developed and refined a multidisciplinary unit on the Harlem Renaissance, connecting her classroom to the larger school and outside community. Irma and I worked together to make her unit public, and in so doing we created a representation of how she, her students, her colleagues, and her neighbors enacted a locally defined conception of a learning community.

GOING PUBLIC WITH LYONS'S CLASS:
DOCUMENTING A LEARNING COMMUNITY

The Harlem Renaissance was a vibrant period of creative artistic, political, and literary innovation in the early decades of the 20th century in and around New York City (Schomburg Center, 2001). It was an era of not only individual achievement but also mutual inspiration and collaboration among seminal artists such as Zora Neale Hurston and Langston Hughes, Billie Holliday and Duke Ellington, and many others. Emerging media— magazines, music publishers, and political organizations' manifestos— supported and advanced these interconnections (Lewis, 1997).

CONTENT FOCUS: EMULATING THE COMMUNITY OF THE HARLEM RENAISSANCE

Irma Lyons was inspired by the model of artistic and intellectual inspiration and collaboration in the Harlem Renaissance and created a multidisciplinary unit to invite her students to step into the lives, achievements, and legacies of individuals from the period. She also saw the unit as a way to expand investigations of African American history beyond the boundaries of its ostensible focus during the month of February. The focus of her scholarship of teaching included exploring the ways in which students might be able to represent richer, more grounded knowledge and expertise than would be suggested by their scores on standardized tests.

PRACTITIONER GOALS

Lyons viewed the outcome project of the unit—a day-long performative "Harlem Renaissance Museum"—as an opportunity for her students to demonstrate their knowledge and expertise as learners. This belief—that multiple measures of student achievement may provide richer and more substantive assessments of student knowledge than iterative standardized tests—undergirded Lyons's inquiry into her teaching practices as a scholar in the Carnegie Academy for the Scholarship of Teaching and Learning (CASTL). Our documentation would aim to mirror this complexity and make it public for interested audiences.

DOCUMENTATION OF THE HARLEM RENAISSANCE MUSEUM PROJECT

Preparing for the Day

On the morning of March 27, 2001, I visited Will Rogers Learning Community Elementary School. As I entered Lyons's classroom, I saw several of her students gathered around computers putting the final touches on their PowerPoint presentations about "their Harlem Renaissance person."

Others spread out life-size paintings of musicians and writers and carefully lettered their names at the top. Lyons moved from one group of desks to the next, helping students with their individual and small-group work. She asked one of her students, Marley, to give me a tour of the classroom and describe the different student projects that would make up the Harlem Renaissance Museum the following day. As we walked, Marley pointed to different children at their desks and explained their projects:

> MARLEY: She's painting a picture of her person, like, see? We're doing it like that little painting over here. We go there, and get something that our person does, and paste it on.
>
> DPM: So, I see a camera on this one. Carl Van Vechten was a photographer?
>
> MARLEY: Yeah. Then these are the timelines of our person—when was he or she born and when he or she died. This is a book jacket, like a hardcover book jacket. We have to put when he was born, what did he do, who he got married to, career, who inspired him. This is the backdrop—we have to draw a picture of our person. We just used regular paint, but this boy right here? He used water paint and crayons. This is a binder to put all the stuff that we found. We had to go on the Internet for research, go in, and type this up. Here's my introduction, early life, education, career, end of life, and bibliography.

After Marley's brief review of the students' works in progress, I circulated around the classroom and spoke with some of the individuals whose work Marley had pointed out. One of these students, Ariana, said that the unit was changing her mind about learning history:

> Learning this will help us to learn in a different way. We're having a fun time learning history, like about this time in history. There's not a lot of people in our class who like to learn social studies, so this is a way to have fun learning about it. When you write your report, you can look on the Internet, and then say a monologue. The work is hard, but you have fun working. She puts on music, and lets us have fun while we're working—but she's *serious* about our work, so we have to get our work done.

On that first day I was in her classroom, Lyons's "seriousness" was not one of somber affect, but of dedicated and energetic contact with each of the students as they put the final touches on their work for the following day. Many of the students remarked that they had attended the Museum with their classes in years prior, and that on those occasions the students "were really descriptive" in their monologue performances. One girl commented with amusement that when she was in second grade, she was very impressed with Lyons's students and wondered, "How did these people get all this? They must have worked since the beginning of school, because it was *too* much!"

While they hadn't actually worked since the very beginning of the school year, the unit did span over 2 months' instructional time and incorporated multiple subject areas. Among the many components of the unit, Lyons's students had not only completed the tasks that Marley described, but had also authored mathematics word problems about the lives of their subjects; superimposed ordered pairs on a grid map of Manhattan; analyzed photographs of their subjects while learning about light, composition, and aperture; painted life-sized portraits; and engaged in intensive literacy-based reading, writing, and oral language development showing their expertise about their subjects' lives. All these components would be on display in the Harlem Renaissance Museum the following day.

Performing the Harlem Renaissance Museum

The next morning I arrived in Room 507, which was buzzing with excitement. Marley and a friend stood in a corner wearing sportcoats and straightening (or unstraightening) each other's ties. A mother fussed over her daughter's "Billie Holiday" finger-waved hairdo. Students gathered in groups rehearsing their monologues in hushed and not-so-hushed tones. Lyons clapped her hands to still the class voices and asked the students to gather the props for their monologues and follow her over to the Will Rogers "Cafetorium," a large high-ceilinged double-duty room that provided space and a stage for assemblies, as well as feeding the entire student body at breakfast and lunchtime. At Lyons's call, "Langston Hughes" grabbed her manual typewriter, "Duke Ellington" his toy piano, and "Augusta Savage" a small ball of clay, and the whole group filed out of the classroom. When they entered the Cafetorium, the students saw that the vertically folding lunch tables, normally pushed against the walls, were arranged in long rows, and each of the upended tables was hung with the students' life-size portraits of their subjects. Any wall space not taken up by tables and paintings was covered with "Harlem Renaissance Timelines" and "Harlem Renaissance Word Problems," and there was a table presenting the students' finished and bound research projects. Shouts of "Wow!" "Sweet!" and "Cool!" erupted as Lyons asked them to gather around her for a "knowledge cheer" in advance of the first class visit of the day. After putting all their hands into the circle, the whole group yelled, "Heeey, knowledge!" cheering and clapping before moving to take their positions in front of their portraits. And not a moment too soon, because the first groups of other Will Rogers classrooms were lining up to come in.

Capturing Multiple Perspectives on the Harlem Renaissance Museum

Over the next 2½ hours, the Cafetorium bustled with museum visitors. The entire population of the school came through in class groups, along with more than 100 visitors from the community—former Will Rogers students and their parents, parents from other classrooms, school board members, and neighbors from the blocks around the school. During this time, I saw broad smiles on the faces of students and parents alike as the Harlem Renaissance "experts" cycled through their monologues for the visitors. I worked my way through the crowd, conducting dozens of quick interviews to try to capture the connections between the audience members and Lyons's students. There were far too many connections than would be appropriate to detail here, so I'll follow one thread outward from a student monologue about the poet Langston Hughes to illustrate how these community connections were nested and interrelated.

Community connections at the museum . In 2001, Lyons's student Dominique had been assigned the role of Langston Hughes. Hughes was one of the most prominent and prolific artists associated with the Harlem Renaissance (Rampersad, 2002) and the author of some of American literature's most recognizable lines; the opening stanza of his 1951 poem "Harlem" gave Lorraine Hansberry the title of her 1959 play, *A Raisin in the Sun.*

For her monologue, Dominique had dressed the part of the dapper Hughes, slicking her straight black hair back from her face and wearing a vest and tie. She sat at a table with several of Hughes's poems on sheets of paper in front of her and confidently began her monologue when approached by a new group of museum visitors.

> My name is Langston Hughes. I was born in Joplin, Missouri, February 1, 1902. My parents were James Nathaniel Hughes and Caroline Hughes. They got divorced soon after I was born. My father moved to Mexico and my mother moved to Lawrence, Kansas, where I was raised by my grandmother. I went to high school at Central High. I went to college at Columbia University, majoring in engineering. As a B+ student, I soon dropped out to pursue my first love—poetry. I finished college 3 years later at Lincoln University, getting a Bachelors of Arts degree. I moved to

Harlem in 1927. I wrote my first book, *Weary Blues*, in 1926. I wrote
my second book, *Fine Clothes to the Jew*, in 1927. I wrote children's
poetry, essays, short stories, novels, poetry, and much more. I
wrote my last book, *The Panther and the Lash*, in 1967, the year that
I died from cancer. I wrote a lot of poems, like "Life Is Fine," "June
the Third" and "Weary Blues." Today I'll read "Life Is Fine."

Dominique reached for one of the sheets on the table in front of her and
proceeded to give an expressive reading of the poem. Her father, not a
native English speaker, was especially proud of his daughter's reading and
speaking skills. After Dominique finished her recitation, I asked him what
he thought about her performance.

She's really prepared for this! I gave her one of my ties so she can
be Langston Hughes. She prepared a *long* time for this. She's really
into it, you know, and she taught me about it, about Langston
Hughes, she read me his poetry, poems, all that. So I enjoyed it, I
learned a lot about this than I knew before, because I haven't
really been into this. I feel great! I feel like she's really involved,
growing mentally and intellectually, and learning about American
history, especially Black history. I think she's matured a lot
through this, when she present her poem from Langston Hughes to
me, she read it like adult. She's matured through this process. I feel
very grateful for Mrs. Lyons.

Dominique listened and then echoed what her father said about their roles
of teacher and student being reversed:

This felt different 'cause usually he teaches me stuff. Usually he's
the one who's telling me things, like math, and things like that.
But this time, I got to teach him. I learned a lot about Langston
Hughes, that he was a great poet, and all about his life.

In this interchange, the learning community begins: two people, father and daughter, reexamining what it means to learn from and with each
other. Dominique's father moved on, circulating around the room, listening to other students' monologues, and a new audience came up to
Dominique's table. This new group included Sharada, a high school student and former student of Lyons, and her mother, Renee. Sharada was
most eager to see Dominique's monologue, because 7 years earlier, she'd
also "been" Langston Hughes. After Dominique finished, Sharada congratu-
lated her on her performance and described what she'd learned from her
own preparation:

When I was Langston Hughes, I had a typewriter, I had pictures up. . . . It's a neat idea. I really see the impact on other children. . . . For me, [it was] learning about different cultures. When I was first in Ms. Lyons's class I didn't know anything about the Harlem Renaissance. I found out not only about Langston Hughes but other people, so that was great. We spent so much time learning about the Harlem Renaissance, everybody learned something different. Even though I'm African American, I still didn't know anything about the Harlem Renaissance, and other people didn't know either, so we were all in the same boat.

Renee nodded as Sharada spoke and then commented that each child developing his or her own expertise contributed to the development of community knowledge:

To see a student's vision come alive, it's *powerful*. To be part of the vision is just something that it's hard to find words to say the impact that it has on you, your own understanding of kids. The historical moment has so much global significance. . . . How do you connect this moment in time, which focuses on African Americans, and make it culturally relevant? . . . [This] group of African Americans have left their mark in so many different areas. It's still prominent, their words, their ways, their stories are still being told! If you could get this sort of collective work going with everything, just think about what education would be like! The sense of community that this activity builds is phenomenal. Not only the teacher learning that went on, but the parent learning, the child learning, and the *reciprocal* learning, that was going on. It's amazing!

But parents and their children were only part of the audience for the museum. The entire population of Will Rogers—35 classrooms in all—cycled through the Cafetorium that day. One of Lyons's faculty colleagues offered her perspective on how Lyons worked to form and sustain this community and described the the schoolwide impact of the Museum:

When you think about it, there are 700 children in this school who'd maybe go to college without ever hearing about the Harlem Renaissance. There are 35 classrooms in this school, and every classroom goes back and has a more detailed discussion about it and engages in conversations: Who was Nella Larsen? What did Cab Calloway contribute? These conversations *never* would have happened without Irma and her inclusiveness of everybody in the

community. It's so powerful. She's changed the culture of our
school. I know that's the big rhetoric, but I can say honestly, more
than anyone else here at Rogers, Irma has done it. It's been a
struggle for her—when she first started, she was met with resistance,
not necessarily from staff, but from parents, from community—why
the Harlem Renaissance? Why not colonialism? But in her humble,
quiet, and powerful way, she's managed to change people's thinking without them realizing they're changing. *That* is the power of a
tremendous leader.

The principal of Will Rogers at the time, Maureen Bradford, echoed the
outcomes of launching and sustaining schoolwide change, as well as the
small changes in the children themselves.

When we were first thinking about these kinds of performances for
kids, we thought, How can we possibly do this? How can we
possibly have every child have an audience to demonstrate their
learning? What we've found is that when you have a community
event like this, it's great because then all of the kids get to demonstrate their knowledge to a lot of different people. They will keep
this with them for a long time to come, not only the facts that they
learned, but also the sense that they *can* learn these things, and
learn them well. That's almost more important, that they see
themselves as learners, as people who can demonstrate their
knowledge to others.

This observation about the inspiring outcomes of the Museum—that students can come to regard themselves as capable learners—was revealed
by many on that day. One teacher from a nearby high school remarked
that she could envision a direct application of the Museum approach to
her own school context:

Oh, this is so inspiring, I have gotten a great idea from Irma. At
my school, we're going to have an extravaganza, and I was going
to have my students become scientists, mathematicians, or
inventors, because we're a math science magnet. I never had
thought about having them all in the same room, in this fashion.
We even have these kind of benches! Irma, we're gonna do the
whole thing. It's gonna be just like this, it's gonna be organized,
I'll have to give you credit, up on the wall: "Inspired by Irma
Lyons!" We'll become the scientists, mathematicians and inventors, and we'll do it like this. I just love this idea! . . . All of the

students I got to hear already have known a lot about the person that they're studying. It's interesting: they're only fifth graders, but they're getting deep knowledge by having names of people that a lot of students are never exposed to, and some only are exposed to when they get to high school. I teach literature in high school, AP English, as a matter of fact, so we have actually read some of the books, and it's nice that they're doing something about the person's life story. When they get to high school and they get to literature, they'll already know these people!

These interconnected stories provide only one strand of the multiple perspectives captured that day. They show how the members' observations and inspirations connected to each other. This inspiration carried over long after the Harlem Renaissance Museum drew to a close at 11:30 a.m.; the Museum had to turn back into a cafeteria in time for lunch.

Community reflections after the Museum. After the Cafetorium had emptied of all people but Lyons and her students, she gathered them back together for another group cheer, hands in the center of a circle: "Grrreeeaaat *job*!" The various Harlem Renaissance musicians stood together in a spontaneous "jam session," miming dramatic performances on their toy saxophones, trumpets, and pianos. "Duke Ellington," a round boy with a thin penciled-on mustache, jumped up and down as he bubbled over to his friends, "We won! It's like, this was a game, and we won the game!"

After the class returned to Room 507, they found a large paper "quilt" of drawings and thank-you statements left on their blackboard by a first-grade class. Lyons read some of them aloud to the class:

Thank you for your hard work, I like all of your art.

Thank you for memorizing. I learned that fifth graders can do a lot.

I was impressed how you do that. Thank you for the information.

Today I learned you can do whatever you want! I was very impressed with your art, thank you.

Today I learned that Josephine Baker had 12 children. I was very impressed with the speeches.

I am impressed that kids are being the real people, like Augusta Savage. I thank you for doing hard work and very good art reports.

Before she'd finished reading the rest of the first-graders' quilt squares, a second-grade class knocked on the door and filed in. Their teacher wanted them to present their own set of reflective responses on the Harlem Renaissance Museum. She addressed Lyons's students as a group:

> My class was *so* impressed with your presentation this morning. They wanted to make you cards to thank you for coming out into our community and teaching us about the Harlem Renaissance. You did a *fabulous* job, very well done. Everybody was so professional, and so knowledgeable, and so eager to share.

After the second graders had gone, Lyons turned to her students and said, "What do you think of that? I was going to have you guys come back to the classroom and do a reflection, but before we even had a chance to do that, you pointed out the card on the board, and then this class came to thank us in person! What does that make you think about?" One of her students replied that she was surprised that students from one class came back to listen to her monologue more than once, taking notes for their own research. Another said that it was fun to see everyone's parents so excited. Some slumped down in comically feigned exhaustion and joked that they were relieved it was over. But most students seemed to sit a little straighter, speak a little more confidently, and talk about each other's work more knowledgeably than they'd done even the day before. They'd come through the event together and were stronger for having done so.

CREATING A MULTIMEDIA REPRESENTATION OF LYONS'S TEACHING

After the Museum day was done, Irma Lyons and I talked. We both were struck by how many connections had surfaced among the presenters and the audience members. We knew that we wanted to make the collection of on-the-spot interviews accessible, present selected examples of the unit curriculum, and describe how Lyons's beliefs about learning in community informed her practices. But we needed a frame to bring these components together. Lyons spoke about how powerful it was just to look across the Cafetorium that morning and see such a vibrant display of community diversity—of age, race, culture, language—all of us gathering around to celebrate a time of innovation and mutual inspiration in Harlem nearly a century before. Together, we began to develop the idea that the multimedia representation of her teaching could present a "community collage" to show the diversity of the people who'd participated in the Museum. Just as the

Harlem Renaissance had gained momentum and publicity from the available media of the time, we could harness the capacity of multimedia and online technologies to take this community to new audiences.

We brainstormed that we could organize the video clips with stills of the interviewee's faces, so that a quick scan of the images would support this goal. In the weeks that followed, I created an interactive image map of the interview video stills, in which moving the computer mouse over the image would reveal a larger image of the video, a description of the clip's contents, and related videos below. So moving the mouse over a picture of Dominique giving her monologue, for example, was linked to her reflections, to other student monologues, to her father's perspective, and to Sharada's response. Clicking on Renee's image linked to Sharada, Dominique, and other former parents. By rolling the cursor arrow over the faces in the grid (Figure 6.1), audiences could learn about the content of the day and the connections between its participants.

We also wanted to provide context for her work prior to the Museum by including an introduction to her classroom, a description of the unit as a whole, a statement of Lyons's beliefs, and an explanation of her philosophy of community learning. Lyons authored these documents and we linked

Figure 6.1. Screen shot of Irma Lyons's MRT.

them from the main collage page. The representation of her practice completed, Lyons could now begin to think about audiences for this community work. Much to her surprise, she herself was her own primary audience.

HOW LYONS'S PRACTICE CAN BE USED
FOR TEACHER LEARNING AND DEVELOPMENT

Looking at the finished website brought new insights for Irma about her
own practice. By engaging in collaborative conversations about how to
frame her work, Lyons articulated links between her classroom community "renaissance"; its Harlem inspirational roots; and, through its own
generative educational power, the larger Santa Monica community.
Through her bringing artifacts from her practice together with the lived
events of the Museum, Lyons observed, the whole became more than the
sum of its parts, beginning to reveal the "soul of her work":

> Being a teacher, when you share your work, you have artifacts—
> here is this picture, here is this photo, here is this—but it can't
> come *alive*. You can't get at the soul of my classroom community
> through the flat two-dimensional text, or photo, or drawing, or
> painting. I think that's what the website has enabled people to do,
> is get into the soul of my classroom community, and my school
> community, with the Harlem Renaissance Museum. It's not about
> the pieces—if they want the text, the text is there, but if they want
> to get the *essence* of my class, they can also hear from a student,
> they can hear from a parent, they can hear from a former student,
> former parents, they can hear from the principal, they can hear
> from the community members that attended.

Not only was she able to share the core of her practice, but she moved
into a stance of critically evaluating and refining her work:

> When you look at yourself on video, when you hear your words,
> you can look at it in a way, in the context that, "Wow, I didn't
> realize that that's what I was doing! You know what? Maybe my
> line of questioning should be a little more . . . or maybe I should
> have pursued this a bit further, when that student asked this
> question." You get to see the small nuances in your classroom that
> you would take for granted. You're now looking at a video *and*
> you're doing a critique on that video, which happens to be of you!
> It's a paradigm shift—from researcher to teacher, from teacher to
> researcher. Because you're right there, in the moment of teaching,

but you're also outside researching yourself, looking at your
practices. That critical lens is amazing.

Lyons's capacity to make her "critical lens" public and shared, building on
her own learning, illustrates the fundamental concepts of the scholarship
of teaching—make the wisdom of practice public, invite critique, so that
others may build upon it (Shulman, 2004).

Lyons's colleagues in and out of Will Rogers described how *they* would
build upon the Harlem Renaissance Museum, bringing the content and
the pedagogy into their own classroom settings. They described outcomes
for the students, for the parents, the school, and for the larger community. By making the Museum public for more than just one day, Lyons
created a resource to support her colleagues as they moved from inspiration to action in their local settings.

Irma Lyons's work not only illustratively describes a community, but
also provides a concrete example of how a learning community evolves
and comes together. This impact extends beyond the boundaries of Will
Rogers. There is an initiative in the larger Santa Monica community to
view the city itself as a "life-long learning community" (Jaffe, 1997), and
the website for that organization links to Lyons's MRT. A school, a neighborhood, and a city can learn from the expertise of some of their young-
est citizens. The "reciprocal learning" experience of the Will Rogers
Elementary Harlem Renaissance Museum touched countless members
of these nested communities. Over the nearly 10 years that she ran the
museum experience, Lyons reached many thousands of Santa Monica
citizens; by comparison, the entire population of Santa Monica in 2001
was only around 90,000 (State of California, 2008). In her reflections on
the Museum, Lyons told me that one of the markers of the Museum's
success was hearing from families how many times their dinner conversation revolved around the students' learnings in this unit. Perhaps that's
where a "learning community" takes root and flourishes—one teacher,
one student, one classroom, one performance, one conversation at a time.

QUESTIONS FOR REFLECTION AND CONVERSATION

- How do you define a learning community? To what learning commu-
  nities do you belong?
- Whose perspectives would be essential in describing your learning com-
  munity? How would those perspectives relate to each other?
- What events, people, or artifacts might you place on a relationship grid?
  How could you make visible the threads of connection between them?

CHAPTER 7

The Noyce Collaborative:
Looking into and Across Practices

E VERY DAY, teachers gather together to engage in after-school workshops or day-long "in-services" intended to improve their classroom practices. But any two in-services can look very different from each other. The label *professional development* is applied equally to one-shot "tips 'n' tricks" exchanges and to intensive, longitudinal, transformative experiences. Professional development, though well intentioned, is often perceived by teachers as fragmented, disconnected, and irrelevant to the real problems of classroom practice. Fewer than half of National Board–certified teachers are satisfied with the quality and quantity of professional learning opportunities available at their school (NBPTS, 2001). Only 42% of teachers surveyed in a study of school leadership felt that their principals provided adequate professional development opportunities (Metropolitan Life/Harris Interactive, 2003).

In 1999, the Noyce Foundation attempted to transform this vision of professional development with an initiative called Every Child a Reader and Writer (ECRW). The mission of the Noyce Foundation is to "improve literacy achievement for students in K–5 utilizing the key strategies of system-wide professional development, classroom coaching and assessment of student work" (Noyce Foundation, 2007a). For a local initiative, they had a large impact: over 7 years, the ECRW project engaged 74 schools in 12 districts to transform teachers' practices in the teaching of writing. Teachers who had participated in ECRW reported back that their practices were significantly reshaped, they had recommitted themselves to creating young writers, and they had even begun to view themselves as writers (Noyce Foundation, 2008b). But by 2006, although they were 6 years into the project, they had relatively few means of showing what this impact looked like in classrooms.

Jennifer Myers, whose work is described in Chapter 5 of this volume, was a teacher whose writing workshop practices were significantly influenced by her school's participation in ECRW. Her MRT was created as a part of the Carnegie Foundation Quest Project for Signature Pedagogies in Teacher Education. In our documentation of Myers's practice, she spoke enthusiastically about how much the Noyce professional development opportunities in writing instruction enhanced her capacity to reach all her students as individual writers. Moreover, her MRT was eliciting a strong response from teachers around the world who were deeply grateful for images of how a teacher approached literacy workshop instruction. My Quest codirector, Ann Lieberman, arranged for us to meet with the leadership of the Noyce Foundation to offer Myers's MRT and the responses from her online audience. The Noyce ECRW leadership—Ann Bowers, Audrey Poppers, and Alicia Heneghan—met with us in the spring of 2006 and immediately were captivated by the direct connection between their goals as professional developers and Myers's work with her students. Myers had adapted and added nuance to the ideas from ECRW to meet her students' needs. She was not performing any kind of "Noyce script," but in her website showed these educators and advocates a vision of the enacted impact of professional development in writing instruction.

Their immediate response was to speak animatedly of all the other teachers whose work they would love to see similarly captured. In that conversation, we realized that we had an opportunity to create a vibrant "legacy" of the Every Child a Reader and Writer Project, a legacy that would capture the Noyce approach to professional development in the teaching of writing and the ways in which participating teachers variably adapted these practices in different grade levels and school contexts.

GOING PUBLIC WITH THE EVERY CHILD A READER AND WRITER INITIATIVE

Any MRT that we would create with ECRW would be new for us, because we had to invent ways of documenting and representing teaching that could generalize across classroom settings and develop protocols that would be particular to the *practices* rather than the practitioners. Our first step was to get to know the central goals and mission of the Every Child a Reader and Writer program.

About ECRW and Genre Study in Personal Narrative Writing

Every Child a Reader and Writer provided intensive professional development for teachers in four "core" school districts and eight "partner" districts, focused on cultivating capacity within the district to sustain the transformation over time. The model involved work by participating teachers, literacy "coaches" (Noyce Foundation, 2008a), principals, and district administrators. The coaches worked one on one with teachers to improve the latter's writing instruction through observation, joint reflection, demonstration lessons, and attendance at professional development series on different "genre studies" for writing instruction. Many teachers affiliated with ECRW began the year with a unit called "Living the Life of a Writer" (Noyce Foundation, 2008c) to orient students to the writing workshop process, before commencing on particular genres of writing.

Any professional learning opportunity is perceived and implemented in distinct ways by participating faculty; this variability is a strength, not a weakness. Poppers and Heneghan wanted to support the work of ECRW teachers, coaches, and administrators by showing the connections between a mutual professional development experience and its implementation in four different classrooms. We began a conversation with Brenda Wallace, an accomplished teacher and professional developer who led the Noyce genre series on the teaching of personal narrative writing. Wallace was energized by the opportunity to share her own practice and beliefs about adult learning and was intrigued to see the connections between her three day-long in-service seminars and several different classrooms' practices (Noyce Foundation, 2007b).

Participating Teachers

The planning team emphasized that audiences of the ECRW work would want to see evidence from different elementary grade levels and school contexts. We recognized that not all ECRW teachers might want to "go public" with their teaching practices, especially if they were actively engaged in refining those practices. We wanted to have at least one early-grade example, one upper-grade example, and two around first and second grade, where so much intensive work is done to launch students on their writing journeys. Poppers and Heneghan contacted four teachers whom they suspected would open their doors to audiences interested in improving their writing instruction. We invited each of the four to the Carnegie Foundation to explore examples of our past work in creating multimedia representations of teaching and a mock-up showing what the ECRW site might look like. We proposed to document each teacher on a day when she or he was teaching personal narrative writing, and we offered to pay for release time for the teachers to come and contextualize the documentation and collected artifacts in their own words. Two of the teachers had participated in the personal narrative genre study series the year prior. The other two would be participating in it for the first time, and we would focus on them during the days documenting Wallace's series. At the end of our presentation, all four teachers agreed to participate:

- Cyrus Limón, who taught kindergarten at Fiesta Gardens Spanish immersion school in San Mateo, California
- Rachel Rothman, who taught second grade at Glider Elementary in San José, California
- Becky Pereira, who taught second grade at Ponderosa Elementary in Sunnyvale, California
- Mark White, who taught fifth grade at Sunnybrae Elementary in San Mateo, California

The structure of the personal narrative genre study helped us to determine the schedule for documenting the classroom practices. The first 2 days of the professional learning series occurred on October 11 and 12, 2006, and focused on the development of a unit plan for personal narrative writing. The teachers then returned to their classrooms, taught the unit, and assessed its outcomes, returning for the 3rd day of the series celebrating their accomplishments on December 6, 2006. We planned that in those 6 weeks we would visit all the classrooms and capture their writing workshop instruction and related artifacts of practice.

The Documentary Team

The quest to go public with ECRW's practices was not something I embarked on by myself. I worked in close collaboration with five experienced and talented colleagues, each with considerable elementary school teaching experience and ease in using videocameras in classrooms. Matthew Ellinger had worked for many years as an elementary school teacher and principal and had recently completed collaborative work with LiPing Ma documenting a local school's collective work to improve their mathematics instruction (Lampkin, 2006). Rebecca Akin was a Stanford doctoral student who had used multimedia to go public with her scholarship of teaching as a CASTL scholar (Akin, 2005). Dilruba Ahmed had worked for many years as the project manager of the CASTL program and had collaborated with several CASTL scholars to create multimedia representations of their scholarship of teaching (Brown, 2003; Moore, 2003). Leslie Butler was a University of California, Berkeley, doctoral student with experience in museum education and documentary film. Ann Lieberman began her career as a sixth-grade teacher in Los Angeles and for decades has been a national leader in teacher networks, writing several seminal volumes about teachers' professional learning and knowledge (Lieberman, 1986; Lieberman & Miller, 1999, 2004). All of us worked in an intensive collaboration to bring about the parallel documentation of five different interconnected learning environments.

Genre Study: Developing a Unit Plan for Personal Narrative Writing

During the first 2 days of the Personal Narrative unit, Brenda Wallace involved a group of 60 teachers from the core ECRW districts in collaborative work in school site teams. The teams developed unit plans for personal narrative writing tailored to each of their grade levels and participated in personal narrative writing of their own. Throughout the 2-day session, Wallace made frequent reference to "touchstone" texts: children's literature that provided rich and evocative exemplars of personal narrative writing (Wallace, 2006b). She read two such texts repeatedly to the faculty participants: *Whistling*, by Elizabeth Partridge and Anna Grossnickle Hines (2003), and *Do Like Kyla*, by Angela Johnson and James Ransome (1993). Both books pair beautifully rendered illustrations with stories of small, personal transformations: a child learns to "whistle up the sun," and a girl who perpetually emulates her older sister's actions finds that imitation is a two-way street.

As Wallace invited the participating faculty to think about, draft, and elaborate on personal narratives from their own lives, she gradually began to fill out a large "unit plan" matrix on a blackboard. Each teacher completed her or his own unit plan for personal narrative writing and revised it in a school-site-based team (Wallace, 2006a). Throughout, Wallace focused the teachers on the idea of *significance* in narrative writing, stressing that any piece of personal narrative needs to clearly communicate why the excerpt was transformative for the author. On the 1st day, the teachers began to write a first draft about a memory of a "significant" experience, and on day 2 they were asked to revisit the draft to make clear its significance for the reader. As this excerpt from the seminar illustrates, Wallace began by emphasizing the idea of significance, provided a vivid example from a student's writing, and then asked the 60 participating faculty to apply the ideas to their own writing:

> You've reread what you've written, and you've asked yourself this question: "Why does this matter to me? Why is this important to me?" and you began to write about that. That's a challenging question. However, specifically to the unit of study that we're talking about, it undergirds everything, because once you've determined for yourself, "Why is this important? What do I want to say?" you've determined a focus. That focus is going to help you make all of your

subsequent decisions about crafting your piece of writing—what you're going to include, what you're going to delete, the details that will be in there, how you're going to revise it.

Let me share with you another example of a student asking herself this question, and what happened with her. This is a fourth-grade student—it's important to know that she's 10 years old before I read it. . . . Here's what her topic is in her writing notebook:

> "You guys! Kiana's here!" said Jordan. "Hurray!" said my team. They were probably worried—where was I?—because I was late. I was late because I had to go to the bathroom. Our soccer game was in Napa and it was about three minutes from Six Flags. No team decided that we should go there. When I got on the grass, I could feel me kind of sinking into the mud. It was really cold outside, so I went to go and and put on my jacket. When I went to go and look at the other team, I asked some questions to myself. Am I going to die? Am I going to get hurt? Am I going to fall in the mud? I asked myself that because some of the girls on the other team looked like they were 12 years old.

Isn't that great? I love it. I was able to talk with Kiana, and she was asking herself the same question: Why is this important to me? We had just been talking about that in her classroom. Initially, when I sat down to confer with her, it was about the event. She said, "I love soccer. I like this game! I like soccer." . . . But, I would share with her again, as I did with this other student, myself. Maybe it's not the event. So let me . . . see if thinking about the event and your strong feeling about it, strong response to it, helps you explore this idea of why it's important to you. So she said, okay, and she was thinking about it, and she went off and then I went back to her, and here's what she wrote:

> Why is this important to me? It's important to me because I *love* soccer. And it also shows me being brave. Because playing against taller girls kind of scares me. So that is why this story is important. It is the first time that I remember being brave.

Oh! Well that's interesting! We can use her as a teacher now, because not only did she explore why the event was important, but her response to it, her feelings. But now, what's happened is, a theme evolved around being brave. That might happen with your own writing and with your students as well. It could be a strong feeling, or could be a big idea, but what's your *response* to the event? I share these ideas with you because before we move on to thinking about planning a draft, it's important to have some sense of why your writing is important to you.

Over the 2 days of initial work in personal narrative writing, Wallace continued to move like this between the teachers' development of their personal narratives and their unit plans; meanwhile, I was working to develop a protocol that would help us make explicit the connections between Wallace's content and the teachers' classroom practices.

Developing a Documentation Protocol

We wanted our documentation of classrooms to be efficient, to be able to draw clear connections between the teachers' classroom practices and Wallace's professional development, and not to overburden the four teachers. I worked with Alicia Heneghan to craft a list of interview questions for the teachers, some of which they could answer prior to the day of documentation over e-mail, others of which would respond to the events of the documented day (see the Appendix). We recognized that teachers actively construct their craft on a daily basis, and wanted to engage Limón, Rothman, Pereira, and White in conversation about links between their writing instruction and their ECRW professional learning without reducing these links to a one-way causal relationship. We planned for two people to document each classroom on a day when the teacher had planned to focus on personal narrative, and we strategized about what each person would do during the few hours available to us. In each setting, we would capture the teacher and her or his students' actions, perspectives, and supporting materials for the writing workshop. We would record the classroom walls. We would divide our documentation into the ECRW writing workshop components—minilesson, one-on-one writing conferences, students' independent writing, and closure—and document "teachers' talk before and after" the instructional events. Our documentation needed to be organized so that we could gather comparable artifacts from each classroom, and so that audiences could read into and across the four teachers' approaches to personal narrative writing.

DOCUMENTING FOUR CLASSROOM APPROACHES
TO PERSONAL NARRATIVE WRITING

It goes without saying that kindergarten is very different from fifth grade, but two second-grade classrooms are also distinct learning environments.

When we entered the classrooms of Limón, Rothman, Pereira, and White we wanted to honor the complexity and situated practices in each classroom while being able to compare the ways in which each teacher engaged her or his students in the writing workshop process.

Practitioner Goals

In reflecting on the day, each teacher described her or his goals for writing instruction. Some emphasized the acquisition of particular skills or strategies of the craft of writing:

> LIMÓN (kindergarten): At this point in the year, I'm trying to focus more on meaning than anything else: comprehension. Writing Workshop fits into that because they're driven to try and write based on what their drawings say . . . how the pictures can help you think about what's happening in a story.
>
> ROTHMAN (second grade): Today I'm going to introduce the students to visualizing as a strategy for writing. We've been doing that during reading time and we've talked a little bit about visualizing to help us with writing but today we're going to make it very explicit, that while they're thinking about creating a picture in the mind of the reader and helping the reader understand their really important parts of their story, they can use visualizing as a strategy to really envision the actions that are happening in their experience and put that into their story.
>
> WHITE (fifth grade): We're going to be looking this time for beautiful language and the writing techniques that [an author] uses to get her message across. And so we're just really going to be listening to the craft. And then I'm going to model how I'm going to take my writing and . . . take one of her ideas and put it into my own writing, because I'm struggling a little bit with how to write this piece about my mom. . . . Then I'm going to have the students go back to their desks and try the same thing. They're going to try to use one of our Touchstone texts or one of the books we've read as a mentor text and try to either add the craft into their writing or to try something new with that.

The two teachers who had recently attended Wallace's unit design series described conceptual goals explicitly linked to the idea of significance in personal narrative writing:

PEREIRA (second grade): Today in writing workshop I intend to ask the children why the topic they selected yesterday is important to them, and asking them to go to the next blank page in their source book and actually write the why, not continue writing the specific story that they selected but why the topic is important to them.

ROTHMAN (second grade): We [have been] investigating significance in books. They read a lot of books. And we really focused on thinking about our feelings during these experiences and in the books that we're reading. And thinking about how feelings help us to identify really important parts of our stories, and also identifying when feelings change, because that usually is a point of realization for the persons having the experience and it's usually very important. So that was—we really focused on feelings. We feel like the kids can really understand that and have a strong feeling about something that you want to connect to it and then convey the significance of it.

We asked the teachers what they looked for in their writing conferences with students. Because the conferences afforded the teachers an opportunity to do direct teaching to a student at her or his level, their considerations illustrate the developmental continuum of learning to write:

LIMÓN: I'm looking for an attempt at writing—some letters. For some kids, that's totally inventive stuff. For other kids, the idea is that they would be able to start sounding things out at this point.

PEREIRA: I will look, number one, to see whether they're able to identify why the event was important to them, and I anticipate that that actually will be kind of tricky for some of them and then so in my conferences I've kind of been thinking through— I may have to ask why and keep going, well, what's the big deal about that? with some of them to really get them to think deeply about the event that they've selected from their life search and why it's important.

ROTHMAN: Given that a lot of them are trying to focus on stretching out on focus, on stretching out their lead, I want to move them forward and tell them once they've set the scene, you know, now it's time to start building up and getting to those important parts and really help give them a strategy to be able to think through their writing as they go because I think it can be very overwhelming.

Writing Workshop

Minilessons. During the teachers' documented minilessons, each of the four teachers stated her or his goals for the day, modeled exemplars in her or his own writing, and oriented the students toward independent writing work. Limón engaged in very detailed modeling, repeating key concepts and regularly prompting his second-language-learning students to see if they were with him:

> Today we're going to select a book to put there on the wall. Our favorite book, okay? The most excellent book. Okay? The most excellent book that we have. So, now I'm going to teach you how you're going to pick you're books, and how you're going to decide which is your favorite book. Okay? Here I have my folder. Right? Here is my folder. But here I only have one book, the book I'm working on. The book I haven't finished yet, right? So, what I have to do is go and collect my books from my yellow box. And for today, I'm going to use Maria's yellow box for Teacher Limón. Here I have my books. All the books that I've done. And I'm going to get all of them, all the books and bring them here, and we're going to imagine that this is my desk. Okay? I'll sit down here.

With older students, Rothman and Pereira invited their students to try on some of the practices of "real writers."

> ROTHMAN: Today, I'm going to teach you that one way that writers help their readers to understand the books they're making and to make pictures in their minds, is by stopping and visualizing actions while they're writing. . . . I'm going to show you how I did this yesterday with my piece after you went home, okay, because I've been working on my piece, remember? I want you to watch while I show you how I stop and visualize the actions and put them into my story.
>
> PEREIRA: We selected a topic yesterday and in our closing yesterday you told me those topics. . . . Today we're going to ask ourselves the question, though, Why? Why is that event important to us? . . . Why was it an event that you wanted other people to know about? . . . With our book, *Whistling* [by Elizabeth Partridge] . . . we asked ourselves the question, Why was this book written, why did the author spend time working hard on it? and we came up with some ideas. . . . We

said that maybe she had had that experience with her dad, maybe she had gone out into the woods and whistled, but we weren't sure because we weren't the author. But today you *are* the author. *You* are the one that gets to determine, why is it important, why is it a story that needs to be told?

With the oldest children, White engaged his fifth graders in developing and refining their technique as writers, focusing on a picture book by Libba Moore Gray and Raúl Colon (1999).

I want to . . . talk a little bit about beautiful language and beautiful writing techniques. Okay? I don't want you to forget significance in your story but I also want you to think about how you can write a book beautifully to get your message across and to get that lesson across. Today we're going to listen to *My Mama Had a Dancing Heart* one more time, but this time you already know the story. I want you to listen to the language and I want you to listen for beautiful things that [Gray and Colon do] to make this a good story.

After the teachers had completed their minilessons and dismissed the groups to independent work on the students' own stories, they engaged with individual students about the latter's writing.

Conferences. Again, the level of sophistication with which teachers and their students were able to unpack and discuss writing was developmental. In kindergarten, Limón guided students to try out some letters and sounds to elaborate their drawings:

LIMÓN: I like how you said that it has letters, right? What else does it have?
MARTHA: Drawings . . .
LIMÓN: Drawings . . .
MARTHA: And letters!
LIMÓN: Letters, okay. What are you going to do now?
MARTHA: Here I'm going to make my daddy, my family, and when we went to the park, and [inaudible] to the house when we came back.

While in fifth grade, White also engaged with a student on higher-level technical elements of her craft:

WHITE: You read that one piece to me and you have this way of, like, grabbing the reader. I know I just wanted to keep hearing more and more about it. So what are you going to try to work on now in your writing? What are you trying to do to make it better?

CAMERON: Well, probably a bunch of stuff, like spelling. Sometimes I write and I, like, leave out words, so I read through them and the spelling too and paragraphing.

WHITE: Okay. And how about techniques? Is there anything that you remember that one of the authors did that you liked, that you want to try in your book?

CAMERON: Um, beautiful language and similes.

WHITE: You're going to try to add some similes. You had some similes. . . . I can see that that's very descriptive, very beautiful. Kind of like what Libba Moore Gray did with lots of words to describe something. Right?

CAMERON: "Alexa slapped her alarm clock like it was an old mother's baby."

WHITE: [laughs] Excellent. All right. So you're going to try to add some similes and you're going to try to add some beautiful language and then you're working on some of your conventions. Excellent.

CAMERON: I have 18 pages. I'm not going to finish it by today, for sure.

WHITE: That's okay—I know you have a great story going here. Now, I think the key is to try to pick out different techniques each day to try to add to your writing to make it even better.

Interviews. Because our team members doing the documentation were all experienced teachers, we were all comfortable engaging students in conversation about their writing. We found that students from each classroom were able to voice profound observations about their work as writers. In Cyrus Limón's classroom, we asked a student what he thought about when he was writing:

DP: what do you think about when you're writing? How do you decide something that you're going to write about?

ELI: I just think of it first, with my pen, with my pen on my chin . . .

DP: You think of it with your pen?

ELI: No, I think about it with my pen on my chin.

DP: Oh, yeah? Can you show me?

ELI: Yes. Like this. [Figure 7.1.]

DP: Awesome. And so do you draw the pictures first, or do you write the words first?

ELI: I write the words first, and then, once I look at the words, I know what I'm going to write, so that's why I write the words first.

Figure 7.1. A kindergarten writer reflects on his writing process.

DP: That's awesome. What's your favorite thing about writing?

ELI: Um, it's about that whenever I write far away from home, or close to home but not in my home, it makes me feel better once I draw a picture of my home, it makes me feel like I'm, I'm really for real at my home . . . really, I'm just at school and I made a picture.

DP: So is it, like, writing helps you imagine your home?

ELI: Yeah.

In Rachel Rothman's second grade, a student talked with my colleague Matt Ellinger about her work to "stretch out" the ideas in her story. Pictures are still a part of the story, as with Limón's student, but the second grader is shifting her emphasis into the written text:

CHELSEA: The first time I started I was sketching out a picture and sketching out and I was about to color them but my teacher said not to. She said to write some down and I stretched the first part and I stretched the middle part out. And now I'm trying to stretch out this part because it's getting to the end part so I can tell when they've broken it. [Figure 7.2.]

ME: I just have one more question for you. Sorry to take up your work time. What does "stretch it out" mean?

CHELSEA: "Stretching out" means—"stretching out" means that you stretch it out and tell them a lot about this page. So you stretch it out so, like, you make the person who's reading it really feel like they're in the story. So I stretched it out on this page.

Figure 7.2. A second-grade writer in process.

By the time the students were in fifth grade, they were able to engage in rich conversations with each other about their writing:

CAMERON: It was the end of Halloween and they were on their way to Sally's house to get ready to count their candy they had got during trick or treating. Alexis had 35 pieces of candy and Sally had 40. But if you're not looking at the thing, at the paper, it— you can't tell if it's another paragraph. I don't know how to . . . When I finish it do I have to make another paragraph?

ALEXIS: You never say, like, another paragraph. Why does the reader—like, if someone's reading to you why do they have to know it's another paragraph if you say, Alexis had 35 pieces of candy and Sally had 40?

CAMERON: Because when you're reading, like, a regular book and you could—I don't know—like, when they change paragraphs, if I'm reading to you and they change paragraphs, you can kind of tell that there's another paragraph going on. But in mine, you can't tell. I don't—I don't think you can tell.

ALEXIS: You want them to tell?

CAMERON: Yes. I want them to tell. When I say this it's, like, a whole different setting. Like, it's saying that—their candy they got during trick or treating. Alexis had 35 pieces of candy. Should I, like—should I add that I have, like—like, when they got back to Sally's house? I don't know, I don't know what to say.

ALEXIS: So they're, like, at someone's house in there?

CAMERON: Yeah. They're—yeah, because you usually count candy—

ALEXIS: Yeah, well, maybe—I think they—someone would figure that. But I think if you want to add it on you can, like, maybe say, when they got back to Sally's house they counted their candy and Alexis has 35 and Sally had 40, something like that.

CAMERON: Should I, like, add it in, but should that be another paragraph?

ALEXIS: Yeah, because they're in a different setting. So maybe you can add that on and it can still be in the paragraph.

CAMERON: And I'd say, like, when they got back to Sally's house and finished counting, Alexis had 35 pieces of candy and Sally had 40.

ALEXIS: Yeah.

CAMERON: Oh, thanks.

Later, White elaborated this peer conference with commentary reminding audiences that peer conferences like this on students' writing don't "happen automatically. It takes a great deal of modeling, praising, and reminding throughout the year to get students to this stage, but the results are powerful."

Reflecting on the Documented Practices

After each day in the teachers' classrooms, the documentary team came together to talk about the writing workshop practices we'd seen. As experienced teachers, we could tell that the use of a consistent protocol to document each classroom was enabling us to look comparatively and developmentally at four different teachers' practices. Our observations were not enough, however. We wanted to ensure that Limón, Rothman, Pereira, and White could describe and provide commentary for each event documented in their classrooms.

Miniconvening: Describing and Explaining Artifacts of Practice

Because only Rothman and Pereira had participated in the 2006 unit design days, we wanted to reproduce the 3rd day of the series with these four teachers, whereby Wallace engaged the larger group in a collective conversation and celebration of their personal narrative units. Teachers shared observations of their student's progress, reflections about how to further refine the personal narrative unit, and preparations for the next ECRW genre study on nonfiction writing.

It was critical to the validity of our work and its grounding in teachers' voices and lived experiences that the participating faculty review all the documentation of their classrooms and provide descriptive and explanatory commentary. We invited them to the Carnegie Foundation for a 2-day miniconvening to engage in this work. Each teacher had her or his own workstation and a DVD of the clips from the classroom, divided into comparable segments: the minilesson, writing conferences, interviews with individual children, and practitioner reflections. We asked Limón, Rothman, Pereira, and White to watch each video clip and craft one pithy paragraph describing what was going on in the video and another paragraph commenting on the place of that clip in their pedagogy or insights that occurred to them upon watching the video.

All the teachers remarked that looking closely at their practice as well as the practices of their colleagues expanded their understandings of writing instruction in their classrooms. Limón commented that seeing how students 2 and 5 years older approached their writing helped give him a longer-range vision of student outcomes, while the teachers of older students remarked that it was helpful to see that even kindergarten students (in the first two months of school, no less) were capable of writing, revising, and conferencing about their work.

CREATING A FRAME TO LOOK ACROSS CLASSROOM PRACTICES: TELLING FIVE STORIES AT THE SAME TIME

Once we had all our artifacts—documentation from the four classrooms and Wallace's 3-day series and descriptions and commentary from all the teachers—we could begin to approach putting these artifacts into a frame. For the first time in our work going public with teaching, we would shift our emphasis from one on individual practitioners to one of shared practices. The documentary team debated how best to accomplish this. We were clear that any artifact represented on the site would always be accompanied by its explanatory description and a commentary, as well as any related materials, such as student work samples, images of classroom walls, and teachers' lesson plans. We were less sure how to visually reinforce the interrelatedness of the four teachers' approaches to writing instruction.

The central components of the ECRW teachers' practices were the events of their teaching captured in video. We needed to show how these events related to each other and create a visual design that would invite audiences to explore into and across these classrooms. In a meeting one day, we sketched out a matrix to tabulate how many video clips we had from the various teachers' classrooms. The numbers differed: we had three writing conferences from Cyrus Limón's classroom, five from Becky Pereira's room, four from Rachel Rothman's room, and six from Mark White's class. But the *category* pertained to each teacher's practice. In that conversation, the documentary team established that we could create categories that could constitute a visual matrix: Opening the Writing Workshop, Students with their Writing, Teachers with their Students, Closing the Writing Workshop, and Teachers Talk Before and After.

I looked at various multimedia sites for models we might draw from, especially multimedia features on newspaper websites, because journalistic accounts have to quickly telegraph compelling and succinct "headline" descriptions of any video-based stories. In some cases, the headline would link to a series of linked video stories. We realized that such a format would allow us to respond to the full measure of data we had (three kindergarten conferences, six from fifth grade, and so on) and also keep each video clip brief enough for audiences to review without investing hours of their time. Audiences could use the matrix (Figure 7.3) to learn that they could watch the entire writing workshop for each of the four teachers by moving horizontally across the matrix, or see the same practice in four different classrooms by exploring vertically.

Figure 7.3. Screen shot of matrix for looking into and across events of teaching.

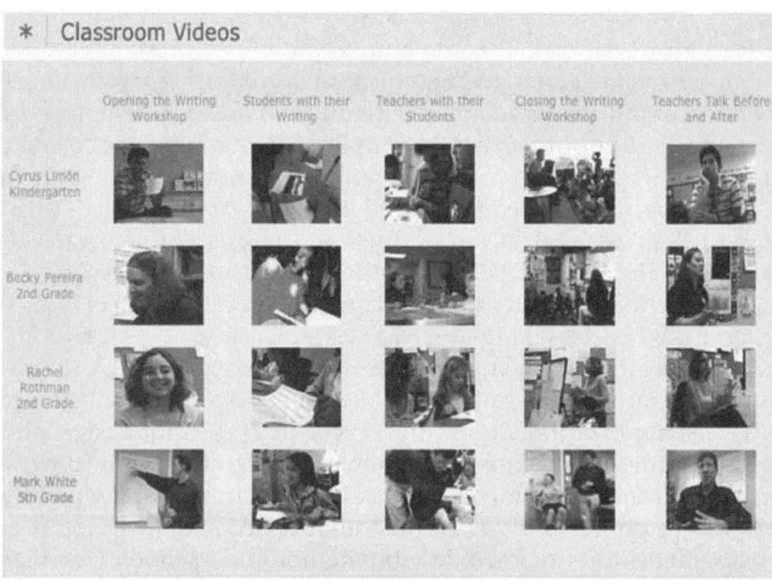

For the individual teachers' videos (e.g., Figure 7.4), we built from some of the conventions of YouTube, assuming that video audiences could watch a video, click on a description, and read a transcription—all at the same time. In each instance, we wanted to remind audiences that the practices represented were nested: Each clip of the minilesson was linked to the others, and each segment of the larger writing workshop was linked to other segments, as well as to the same segment in other teachers' classrooms.

We elicited support for the Flash-based design of the videoplayer and its accompanying tabbed panel of descriptive material from our colleagues in the Carnegie Foundation Knowledge Media lab, who were able to transform our mockup into an interactive reality. We also worked closely with Brenda Wallace, who had the considerable task of not only watching all 18 hours of her own unit design seminar series, but also reviewing the teachers' practices to establish links between the professional learning for ECRW participating faculty and the ways in which Limón, Rothman, Pereira, and White adopted and adapted the concepts of personal narrative writing instruction for their students. Wallace also crafted a lengthy narrative making explicit her beliefs about adult learning, her rationale for approaching the unit design as she did. She also linked to the materials from the professional development sessions and video clips of seminal moments from the 3-day series. Meanwhile, Audrey Poppers and Alicia Heneghan wrote a description of the ECRW project and its central premises for writing workshop instruction so that site audiences would have a context for the larger initiative supporting these five practitioners' work.

By May of 2007, we had finished the frame for the multimedia representation of Every Child a Reader and Writer (Figure 7.5). All the videos were linked; transcriptions, descriptions, and commentaries were proofread. The website, http://www.InsideWritingWorkshop.org, was "live." It was time to field test the finished public site with its preliminary audience: participating literacy coaches, principals, and district administrators.

HOW THE INSIDE WRITING WORKSHOP CAN BE USED FOR TEACHER LEARNING AND DEVELOPMENT

At our initial orientation day for the ECRW coaches, principals, and district administrators, we wanted to take these "insiders" into the practices represented on the site. We showed them the front page, clicked on "Explore the Classrooms," and played a few videos while scrolling through the transcripts and opening related documents. The participating educators immediately remarked about the ways they could envision using the site for teacher development at their school. One literacy

Figure 7.4. Screen shot of linking from one teacher's practice to others.

Figure 7.5. Screen shot of Every Child a Reader and Writer.

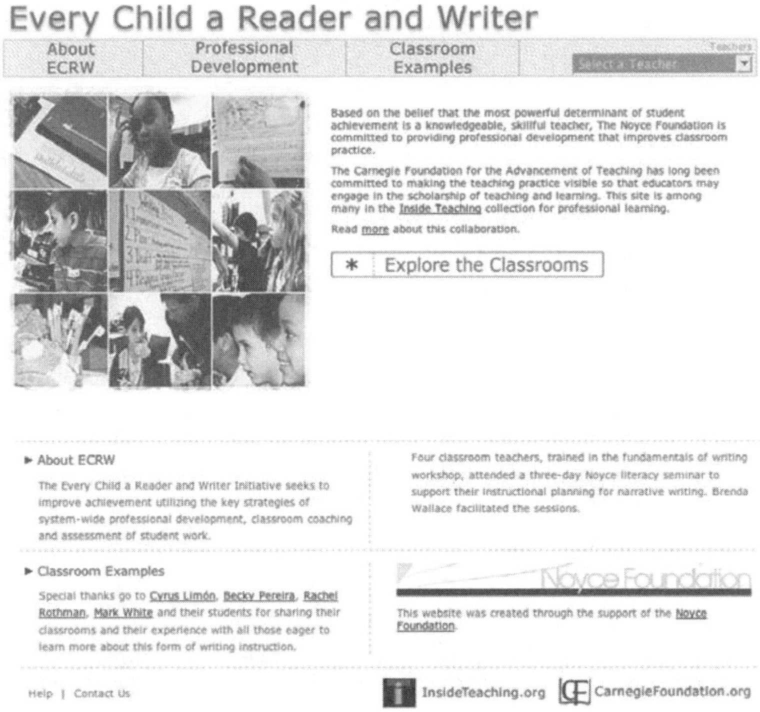

coach described that in her work supporting novice teachers, she takes them to observe their accomplished colleagues, but when they do, the novice teacher only "looks out"—at the walls, the student work samples, the arrangement of the room, the classroom management system—while the coach wants her to "look in" to the interactions between teacher and student, the teacher's planning process, and subtle nuances of the teaching practice that are hard to identify in the moment. This coach shared that InsideWritingWorkshop.org could help her prepare new teachers to observe in their colleagues' classrooms and create a plan to both "look out *and* look in." She said that starting with the lesson plan and the images of the learning environment would address her novice colleagues' interests, and the videos and student writing samples from writing workshop conferences would help her teach them ways to "look in." A principal commented that he would share the site with the entire parent community e-mail list for his school to help parents understand the school approach to writing instruction. He continued that it would "jump-start" back-to-school night by focusing on practices and helping parents see how much information about students' learning was contained in their multiple drafts of a single written composition.

The teacher educators who had found Jennifer Myers's site relevant to their preservice teacher education courses also eagerly embraced InsideWritingWorkshop.org, as it would help emphasize to novice teachers that accomplished teaching practices in literacy were not the personal property of expert teachers. We also found that other faculty working in teacher learning and professional development were inspired by Brenda Wallace's example of accomplished practice; her work to make explicit her teaching, her rationale and her materials provide one of very few examples in existence of multimedia representations of faculty development practices. As Wallace describes in her rationale, every teacher can engage in a process of improving her teaching: "Much of the work of professional development is to lift people up and engage in a process of change, moving from a stance of certainty to curiosity" (Noyce Foundation, 2007b). This process is enhanced by recognizing that looking across classrooms and practices can occasion new and deeper conversations about developing *all* of our young writers' craft.

QUESTIONS FOR REFLECTION AND CONVERSATION

- What practices do you share with your teaching colleagues?
- How might you look into and across these teaching practices?
- What new conversations might you be able to have about refining your collective practices by doing this kind of "work sampling" with the *events* of teaching and learning?

CHAPTER 8

Into Our Own Classrooms:
How Going Public Can Launch and
Sustain a Vibrant Teaching Life

A MONG MY teaching colleagues, I have been privileged to have an opportunity that many teachers crave but few experience: to spend extensive amounts of time in other people's classrooms. Many teacher education programs emphasize the importance of learning from others' practices; Alverno College, where I teach, has five different field placements before our graduates become full-time classroom teachers. But even my own students, once they enter their own classrooms, are too often isolated from their colleagues and cut off from opportunities to learn from the practices of others. It's not surprising that teaching is one of the professions with the highest rates of burnout and "career depression" (Cherniss, 1992).

JOINING A GLOBAL NETWORK OF EDUCATORS

Teachers can challenge that trend, however. My purpose in sharing the work of practicing teachers is to inspire you, not only by sharing the innovative teaching strategies in each of these classrooms, but also by showing how much others can learn from teachers' going public. Terry Loomis, Yvonne Hutchinson, Irma Lyons, Jennifer Myers, and the Noyce-allied teachers have all joined an invisible but growing global network of teachers whose connections do not depend on geographic proximity or time spent after school in teachers' lounges, but on a shared commitment to improving their students' learning by looking closely at their own teaching practices.

This work is not theirs alone. Even in the beginning years of your teaching career, you can seek out answers to challenging problems, compare what you and your students are doing to work in other contexts, and continue to engage in professional discourse around issues of teaching and learning. Instead of beginning your career by closing your classroom door behind you and facing your students alone, you can bring your colleagues into your classroom and begin each day with a foundation of current and ever expanding understandings about teaching. By going public with your own practice and continuing to learn from others' classrooms, you can make visible your own continuum of professional learning (Feiman-Nemser, 2001) and contribute to an expansion of public understanding of teachers' work.

WHERE TO BEGIN?

Images of teachers' work are too often shaped by Hollywood. Movie audiences watch inspirational tales of a teacher beating insurmountable odds to reach her challenging students without any help from her colleagues or administrators—in fact, often working in direct opposition to them. The reality of engaged professional education work, however, shows us that teachers learn powerfully and productively in collaboration with each other and as participants in professional learning communities (Lieberman & Miller, 2008). By thinking carefully about your own teaching, asking good questions, and using the power of multimedia tools to pursue answers to those questions, you can change your experience of teaching.

Thinking About Your Teaching

Every day in our classrooms, things happen that we don't anticipate. Our lesson takes longer or goes faster than we planned, students have questions we never thought of, or forces outside the classroom affect our work within. Curriculum needs to be transformed and adapted; rapidly changing student populations demand that we educate ourselves about cultures and traditions different from our own. From small-scale "Huh!" questions to large-scale critiques, asking questions about our practice is one way of continuing to learn from our teaching. Keeping a teaching journal can help you track your questions over time and connect them to each other (Rust & Clark, 2007). Engaging your students as collaborators can be transformative for you and them (Oakes & Rogers, 2006)— as Anna Richert's Arroyo Day illustrates, you and your students may have very different perceptions of the same teaching and learning events (Richert, 2006).

Documenting Your Practice

It can be daunting to think about creating a large-scale complex multimedia record of your teaching when you feel that your practice is still developing. So don't! Start small, focused, and manageable. Don't videotape an entire 2-week curriculum unit—especially in your first years in the classroom, you won't have the extra time required to review and make sense of extensive and lengthy recordings.

Gather artifacts of everyday teaching. Start by looking closely at artifacts of your teaching: reflective journals, images of student work, notes in the margins of your lesson plans, stick-on notes protruding from your textbooks with comments about your curriculum. Look at your classroom walls. What does the work displayed there and the resources made available to students tell you about the learning taking place? Think about school documents that shape your teaching, such as the School Accountability Report Card or the district website. Examine them for connections to your questions. What might help you get answers to explain a performance gap between groups of your students on an assessment?

Use available multimedia tools. Increasingly, teachers have media tools available to them, even if they don't realize it. Many mobile phones now come with cameras or audiorecording features. If you're circulating around the classroom and see an interesting drawing about the morning's readaloud created by one of your first-graders, stop and take a picture of it, and write briefly on a stick-on note why you found it interesting. Keep your PowerPoints, Interactive WhiteBoard files, e-mails to your colleagues, and interesting bookmarks of web resources that you share with your students. Once a week or so, take a look at the documents you've collected, electronically and otherwise, and see how they advance your learning about existing questions or raise entirely new questions that you might want to pursue.

Getting permission before you go public. You might think about keeping these documents online in a website or blog. This can make your organization easier, as many blogs are automatically organized by date and archived for searching. I want to encourage you, however, to do so only after you have received permission for sharing your students' work in this way from their parents. Many districts and schools now have blanket media releases to cover electronic representations of students' work, but you want to be sure. All the teachers' work in this volume, for example, was gathered with full permission from each of the students' parents. Students whose parents did not grant permission still participated in the classroom sessions, but were seated outside the view of the camera. Be mindful of how you present your work with your students—every teacher vents about frustrations of the job, but you can (and should) avoid blaming your students for the challenges that frame your inquiry.

Sharing Your Practice with Others

Once you have gathered some documents of your teaching and looked at them to learn what answers they provide and what new questions they raise, you can begin to share these insights with your colleagues. Remember that in this digital age, your colleagues might be in the classroom next door, or on a Listserv for other middle school social studies teachers, or attending a district professional development workshop with you. Seize opportunities to learn from others' responses to your questions. Don't be shy about sharing your teaching: I can tell you honestly that I and every teacher with whom I've collaborated have experienced that moment of mortification when looking at ourselves on video for the first time. Instead of presenting documentation of your teaching as an opportunity for others to judge your strengths or weaknesses as a teacher, use it as a chance to engage with others in questions about teaching and learning. Ask your mentor to look at a video of a student writing conference with you, and see if you can identify particular insights the student makes into her or his writing. Ask your teacher friends to look at samples of mathematics assessments and suggest ways to build lessons out of students' own problem-solving strategies. Going public is a way for you to become a better teacher and for your students to learn more from and with you. Keeping your eyes on that prize will help get you over the reluctance to let other people watch you in action. Frame your sharing around questions you have, and the conversations that ensue will be immediately applicable to your teaching.

CHANGING TEACHING BY OPENING OUR DOORS

If educators are to engage in a transformation of public perceptions of the work of teaching, to expand conversations about "great teachers" beyond just a cult of personality, we need to greatly increase the numbers of people who are documenting their teaching, creating innovative frames through which to share practice with others, and engaging in substantive and critical conversations about what can be learned from this collective work. This is work *you* can do: for yourself, to sustain your engagement in the profession, and for others, to learn from your contributions to knowledge about teaching and learning.

Every teacher shares something different about her or his classroom, and every teacher gains something different from going public. We've seen those differences in this book. For Terry Loomis, the multimedia tools her students used to create movies about their home languages and cultures allowed her to see the ways in which she had empowered her students to participate actively in cultural inquiry. For Yvonne Hutchinson, going public allowed her to share her students' rich discussions and the universal human concerns that drove her English curriculum. For Irma Lyons, it meant being able to share the multiple voices and perspectives of the school learning community. For Jennifer Myers, documenting and sharing teaching meant expanding her grade-level faculty collaborations for literacy workshop to include educators from schools around the world. For the teachers participating in the Noyce Foundation Every Child a Reader and Writer initiative, it meant seeing the powerful variability of teachers' adaptations of professional development curricula. What will you share about your own teaching? What do you hope to learn from the teaching of others?

It all starts with you. You make the decision to open your classroom door by using available tools to share your teaching with others. You don't have to be an "expert" in teaching or in technology to share your teaching practices with others. Increasingly, web-based tools such as Blogger and YouTube, as well as such computer-based tools as iWeb, enable people to create and upload multimedia artifacts to the web. The KEEP toolkit (http://www.cfkeep.org) provides ways in which educators can make their practice public as well as linking it to a "commons" for teaching and learning (http://commons.carnegiefoundation.org). You might start by just setting up your digital camera on movie mode and recording one interchange with a student. You might walk next door to your colleague and play it back for her and share your thoughts about what you see happening. Or you might upload the video to TeacherTube.com along with an image of the student work and your reflections about what you see in both artifacts. If a group of your grade-level colleagues do the same, you can engage in new kinds of conversations about your mutual practices. Your school faculty might be able to assess how robust the curriculum is across subject areas and grade levels. Your state superintendent of public instruction might have more meaningful data about teaching and learning to inform her decisions. But we can't have these kinds of conversations if practice stays private. We have to open our doors, and the process starts with each of us. I look forward to learning from *your* teaching!

Documentary Protocol

BEFORE THE DAY OF DOCUMENTATION

Lead documenter collects from teacher:

- Directions to school
- Time of writers' workshop, arrange time for pre- and postinterview
- Location of office, visitors policy
- Personal Narrative Unit Design Matrix
- Lesson plan for documented day
- Names of touchstone texts you're using for writers' workshop unit on personal narrative
- Expanded list of related books for reading time during unit (but hopefully not *too* large a list)

Lead documenter finds out from teacher:

- Is there anything we should know about your school, your class, or your students before we visit?
- Do you want us to introduce ourselves to the principal before coming to your class?
- What are standards for teacher dress at your school? (We don't want to be over- or underdressed.)
- How would you like us to introduce ourselves?
- What students do we need to make sure *not* to videotape on the day we visit? How/where will those students be seated so as to be outside the camera view?
- What students would you like to make sure we videorecord during independent work time? What unplanned events should we be prepared to capture if they arise (e.g., peer-to-peer writing conference requests)

- Are there particular questions you'd like us to ask your students about their writing during independent writing time? How might we get at their understanding of the idea of significance in narrative writing, or other issues related to writing that you want to share with other teachers?
- Are there any other issues you're curious about that we can help you see while we're there?

ON THE DAY OF DOCUMENTATION

Before writers' workshop time (ideally before school, or during recess, times when students are not in classroom):

Documenter A

Interviews teacher:

- What is your plan for your writing workshop today?
- What do you want students to learn? How will you know if they've learned it? (What will you look for?)
- What have you been doing in your *reading* time that prepared students for what you're working on today in writers' workshop?
- What have you been doing in your *writing* time that prepared students for what you're working on today in writers' workshop?
- How have you introduced the idea of significance in personal narrative writing (today and in the larger unit)?
- How have you been modeling these ideas for the students in your own writing?
- What have you seen in student work that informed

Documenter B

- Takes photos of classroom walls, especially charts, posters, student work samples relevant to reading and writing time. Photos should be whole frame as well as zoomed in (like Myers's interactive classroom walls).
- Takes photos of any supports for English language learners.
- Scans lesson plans if not gathered ahead of time.
- If teacher has conferences as a table, takes photo of table.
- Takes photos of where the writing workshop supplies are stored (students' desks? writing folder cabinet?).

your minilesson plan and conferences for today? Is it possible to see that student work, if relevant, and talk through it?
- What have you learned in your conferences that informed your minilesson plan and conferences for today?

During writers' workshop minilesson:

Documenter A

- Camera on teacher.
- Collects any materials shared by teacher during minilesson (teacher's own writing, writing time support documents).

Documenter B

Camera on students.

During writers' workshop independent writing time:

Documenter A

- Follows teacher as she or he conferences with individual students.
- Takes images of anecdotal assessments (stick-on notes, comment charts).
- Takes still photos of student work after each conference.

Documenter B

- Follows students whom the teacher has identified as interesting cases. Asks questions that the teacher has expressed interest in.
- Is prepared to document any unplanned events that arise (e.g., peer conference requests).
- Takes still photos of student work after each. interview.

During writers' workshop closure period:

Documenter A

- Camera on teacher and/or students who are sharing their writing.
- Takes still photos of any work that was shared.

Documenter B

Camera on students who are the "audience."

After writers' workshop, ideally during recess or after school:

Documenter A	Documenter B

Interviews teacher:

On writing workshop:

- What happened today?
- What did you see in your writing conferences with students?
- What surprised you about today's events?
- What changes did you need to make in your plan?
- What do you see in these pieces of student work that were generated?
- Did anything surprise you in the student work you saw today? Why do you think some of those things happened?
- What will you do next in writing workshop? In reading time to support students' writing?
- What are your hopes for this class as writers?

On serving linguistically diverse students:

- What particular considerations have you taken to support the access of your English language learners to the material?
- How did you introduce the idea of significance to your English-language learners?
- What are they learning from you about English-language development during writers' workshop time?
- What are they learning from their peers about English-language development during writers' workshop time?

Documenter B

- Takes stills of anything else in classroom that will help people understand the context and content of the documented events.
- If there is scanner on site, scans images of student work or other related materials.

AFTER THE DOCUMENTED DAY

Ask teacher to respond to the following by e-mail:

Resources:
- What resources (books, colleagues, professional development initiatives) do you draw on for your writing curriculum?
- What resources (books, colleagues, professional development initiatives) do you draw on for your reading curriculum?
- What school, district, state, or national standards guide you in your literacy instruction?

Context:
- School Accountability Report Card (SARC)
- What's your class profile (number of boys/girls, other demographics, number of English language learners, students' English-proficiency levels)?
- What's your curriculum context (open court, pacing guides, English only)?
- Are there any district/school expectations for literacy that people should know about to understand you and your work?

Personal History:
- Why/how did you become a teacher?
- What's your professional history?
- Why/how did you begin to focus on writing?
- What's your history as a writer? What are your strengths? What do you struggle with?
- Who are your favorite writers (for your own reading, for your students)?
- Is there anything else you want people to understand about you and your work that you haven't shared elsewhere?

REFLECTIVE MINICONVENING

Teachers bring:

- Responses to preceding prompts
- Student work samples from unit as a whole, particularly students who were videotaped on the documented day
- Initial reflections from watching video
- Becky and Rachel: what they're looking forward to on Day 3

Teachers do:

- Review video.
- Provide explanatory commentary for each clip and artifact (what would people need to know to understand this piece of my practice?).

Teachers discuss:

- How did your Noyce preparation in significance in narrative writing connect to what people will see in the documentation of your practice?
- What are the ways in which you adapted the "big ideas" from the Noyce days for your classroom?
- What did you do in your teaching of writing before this unit? What came next?
- How have you shared your Noyce work with local colleagues?
- How long has your school been involved in the Noyce project?
- How does your school support your work with Noyce, on site and off site?

References

Aguilar, E. (2004). *An East Oakland odyssey: Exploring the love of reading in a small school*. Retrieved August 14, 2008, from http://gallery.carnegiefoundation .org/collections/quest/collections/sites/aguilar_elena/

Akin, R. (2005). *A narrative in three voices*. Retrieved March 24, 2008, from http: //www.goingpublicwithteaching.org/rakin/

Andrews, M. (2005). *A fifth-grade unit on Colonial New York: Developing perspectives through historic role play*. Retrieved March 10, 2008, from http://www.tc.edu/ ncrest/teachers/andrews/index.htm

Beal, N. (2004). *Teaching art*. Retrieved March 10, 2008, from http://www.tc.edu/ ncrest/nancybeal/nancy.htm

Boerst, T. (2003). *The development and use of Representations in teaching and learning about problem solving: Exploring the Rule of 3 in elementary school mathematics*. Retrieved March 10, 2008, from http://gallery.carnegiefoundation.org/ collections/castl_k12/tboerst/

Brown, V. (2003). *Human agency, social action, and classroom practices: What happens when teachers move over to allow students to pave their own path towards enacting change?* Retrieved March 24, 2008, from http://gallery.carnegiefoundation .org/collections/quest/collections/sites/brown_vanessa/

Burgos, D. (2007). Adaptation and IMS learning design. *The Journal for Interactive Multimedia in Education*. Retrieved March 11, 2008, from http://www-jime .open.ac.uk/2007/01/

Calkins, L. M. (2001). *The art of teaching reading*. Boston: Allyn & Bacon.

Campioni, J. (2007). *Miss Campioni's third-grade classroom website*. Retrieved March 11, 2008, from http://www.misscampioni.com/

Capitelli, S. (2002). *Learning from our conversations in English: Using video in the bilingual classroom as a tool for reflection on English language learning and teaching*. Retrieved November 19, 2008, from http://gallery.carnegiefoundation.org/ collections/castl_k12/scapitelli/

Capper, J. (2002). *Uses of technology to support high quality teacher professional development*. Retrieved March 10, 2008, from http://unesdoc.unesco.org/images/ 0013/001347/134793eo.pdf

Carnegie Foundation for the Advancement of Teaching. (2007). *Inside teaching: A living archive of practice*. Retrieved August 14, 2008, from http://www.inside teaching.org

Carnegie Foundation for the Advancement of Teaching. (2008a). *KEEP toolkit: knowledge, exchange, exhibition, and presentation.* Retrieved August 15, 2008, from http://www.cfkeep.org

Carnegie Foundation for the Advancement of Teaching. (2008b). *Teaching and learning commons.* Retrieved August 15, 2008, from http://commons.carnegie foundation.org/

Center for Digital Storytelling. (2008). *Listen deeply: Tell stories.* Retrieved August 15, 2008, from http://www.storycenter.org

Cherniss, C. (1992). Long-term consequences of burn-out: An exploratory study. *Journal of Organic Behaviour, 13,* 1–11.

Clay, M. (1993). *An observation survey of early literacy achievement.* Portsmouth, NH: Heinemann.

Cone, J. (2003). *Constructing urban high school students as achievers.* Retrieved March 10, 2008, from http://www.goingpublicwithteaching.org/jcone/

Corporation for Educational Network Initiatives in California. (2001). *Digital California Project: Frequently asked questions.* Retrieved March 10, 2008, from http://www.cenic.org/publications/archives/glossies/dcpfaq.pdf

Creative Commons. (2008). *Creative Commons: Share, remix, use—Legally.* Retrieved August 15, 2008, from http://www.creativecommons.org/about/

Davis, V. (2008). *The CoolCat Teacher Blog.* Retrieved March 11, 2008, from http://coolcatteacher.blogspot.com/

Delicious. (2008). *Delicious: Social bookmarking.* Retrieved August 15, 2008, from http://www.delicious.com

Dennis, K. (2008). *My story. StoryCenter.org: Listen Deeply. Tell stories.* Retrieved March 11, 2008, from http://www.storycenter.org/stories/

DePaola, T. (1975). *Strega Nona.* New York: Scholastic.

DePaola, T. (1993). *Strega Nona meets her match.* New York: Putnam.

Dolgonas, J. (2008). *Computer and Internet use in California: Progress and paradox.* Retrieved August 15, 2008, from http://www.cenic.org/publications/cenictoday/Jun08_CT.html

Ellinger, M. (2008). *Multimedia Records of Teaching: A Carnegie convening.* Retrieved March 12, 2008, from http://mrt.carnegiefoundation.org/

Erickson, F. (1982). *Sights and sounds of life in schools: A resource guide to film and videotape for research and education* (Research series). East Lansing: Institute for Research on Teaching, Michigan State University.

Erickson, F. (2006). Studying side by side: Collaborative action ethnography in educational research. In *innovations in educational ethnography: Theory, methods, and results* (pp. 235–258). New York: Routledge.

Erickson, F. (2008). *The classroom ecosystem explorer: Developing and testing a multimedia tool to support early grades instruction in science.* Retrieved March 10, 2008, from http://64.233.167.104/search?q=cache:EHF0lK4YrTEJ:cse.edc.org/drk12/drk12reports/ViewAbstract.aspx%3Fid%3D816+%22classroom+ecosystem+explorer%22&hl=en&ct=clnk&cd=2&gl=us&client=safari

Feiman-Nemser, S. (2001). From preparation to practice: Designing a continuum to strengthen and sustain teaching. *Teachers College Record, 103*(6), 1013–1055

Fountas, I. C., & Pinnell, G. S. (1996). *Guided reading: Good first teaching for all children*. Portsmouth, NH: Heinemann.

Franz, E. (2006). *Personal geometries: Working within the variable landscapes of language, culture, curriculum, and relationship*. Retrieved March 10, 2008, from http://quest.carnegiefoundation.org/~dpointer/ellenfranz

Gardner, H. (1995). *How are kids smart?* [*videorecording*]: *Multiple intelligences (M.I.) in the classroom*. Port Chester, NY: National Professional Resources.

Gardner, H. (1997). *Frames of mind: The theory of multiple intelligences*. Jackson, TN: Basic Books.

Giles, J. (1994). *The flood* (PM Library Green Level 14). Florence, KY: Cengage Learning.

Giles, J. (1997). *The toy farm* (PM Story Books Orange Level 15 Set A). Florence, KY: Cengage Learning.

Goldman-Segall, R. (1996). *Points of viewing children's thinking: A digital ethnographer's journey*. Mahwah, NJ: Lawrence Erlbaum Associates.

Gray, L. M., & Colon, R. (1999). *My mama had a dancing heart*. New York: Scholastic.

Gray, R. (2008). *Welcome to Mrs. Gray's classroom*. Retrieved March 11, 2008, from http://www.genevaschools.org/austinbg/class/gray/

Grossman, P., & Compton, C. (2006). *How do we prepare teachers to lead student-centered, text-based discussions in their classrooms?* Retrieved February 24, 2008, from http://quest.carnegiefoundation.org/~pgrossman/

Hammerness, K., Shulman, L., & Darling-Hammond, L. (2000). *Learning from cases*. Retrieved March 11, 2008, from http://gallery.carnegiefoundation.org/collections/castl_he/khammerness/

Hatch, T., Ahmed, D., Lieberman, A., Faigenbaum, D., White, M. E., & Pointer Mace, D. (Eds.). (2005). *Going public with our teaching: An anthology of practice*. New York: Teachers College Press.

Huber, M. T., & Hutchings, P. (2005). *The advancement of learning: Building the teaching commons*. San Francisco: Jossey-Bass.

Hurley, M. (2001). *Making change visible*. Retrieved March 10, 2008, from http://gallery.carnegiefoundation.org/mhurley/index2.html

Hutchings, P., & Shulman, S. (1999, September/October). The scholarship of teaching: New elaborations, new developments. *Change, 31*(5), 10–15.

Hutchinson, Y. (1998). *Discussing race through "Cora, Unashamed."* American Collection Educator's Site. Retrieved February 24, 2008, from http://www.ncte americancollection.org/cora_issues.htm

Hutchinson, Y. (2003). *A friend of their minds: Capitalizing on the oral tradition of my African American students*. Retrieved March 10, 2008, from http://goingpublic withteaching.org/yhutchinson/

Jaffe, L. (1997). *Santa Monica, a lifelong learning community: The need for a comprehensive look at education* (*call to action paper*). Retrieved March 25, 2008, from http://smllc.org/lllc_background.html

Johnson, A., & Ransome, J. (1993). *Do like Kyla*. New York: Scholastic.

Johnson, B. (2005). *Place-based storytelling tools: A new look at Monticello*. Paper presented at Museums on the Web Conference 2005. Retrieved March 11,

2008 from http://www.archimuse.com/mw2005/papers/johnsonB/johnson
B.html

Keren-Kolb, E., & Fishman, B. (2006, April). *Using drawings to draw out a preservice teacher's beliefs about technology integration.* Paper presented at the annual meeting of the American Educational Research Association, San Francisco.

Kocher, J., & Andrews, W. (2001). *How to survive night class.* Born Magazine.com. Retrieved March 11, 2008, from http://www.bornmagazine.org/projects/nightclass/

Kristeva, J. (1980). *Desire in language: A semiotic approach to literature and art.* (L. S. Roudiez, Ed., T. Gora, A. Jardine, & L. S. Roudiez, Trans.). New York: Columbia University Press.

Kroll, L. (2006). *Connecting assessment with teaching in literacy: How to learn from someone else's practice.* Retrieved March 7, 2008, from http://www.cfkeep.org/html/stitch.php?s=74830473842873&id=53816938916051

Krug, S. (2000). *Don't make me think! A common sense approach to web usability.* Berkeley, CA: Peachpit Press.

Ladson-Billings, G. (1997). *The Dreamkeepers: Successful teachers of African-American children.* San Francisco: Jossey-Bass.

Lampert, M., & Ball, D. L. (1998). *Teaching, multimedia, and mathematics: Investigations of real practice.* The Practitioner Inquiry Series. New York: Teachers College Press.

Lampkin, S. (2006). *Transforming teacher learning to student learning: Pedagogical content knowledge with LiPing Ma.* Retrieved March 11, 2008, from http://gallery.carnegiefoundation.org/collections/quest/collections/sites/lampkin_sue/pckMa.htm

Lawrence-Lightfoot, S., & Hoffman Davis, J. (1997). *The art and science of portraiture.* San Francisco: Jossey-Bass.

Lessig, L. (2006). *Free culture: What we need from you.* Keynote presentation at the annual meeting of Linuxworld. Retrieved March 12, 2008, from http://www.linuxworld.com/events/keynotes/lwsf06–lessig.html

LessonLab. (2008). *Lesson Lab Research Institute.* Retrieved November 18, 2008, from http://www.llri.org/html/research.htm

Lewis, D. L. (1997). *When Harlem was in vogue.* New York: Penguin Non-Classics.

Lieberman, A. (1986). *Rethinking school improvement: Research, craft, and concept.* New York: Teachers College Press.

Lieberman, A., & Miller, L. (1999). *Teachers: Transforming their world and their work.* New York: Teachers College Press.

Lieberman, A., & Miller, L. (2004). *Teacher leadership.* San Francisco: Jossey-Bass.

Lieberman, A., & Miller, L. (2008). *Teachers in professional communities: Improving teaching and learning.* New York: Teachers College Press.

Lieberman, A., & Pointer Mace, D. (2008, May/June). Teacher learning: The key to educational reform. *Journal of Teacher Education, 59*(3), 226–234.

Linden Research. (2008). *Second Life: Your world, your imagination.* Retrieved August 15, 2008, from http://www.secondlife.com

Lyne, H. (2001). *The Mission Hill School.* Retrieved March 10, 2008, from http://goingpublicwithteaching.org/hlyne/

Lyons, I. (2001). *Multiple measures of student achievement in an interdisciplinary unit on the Harlem Renaissance.* Retrieved March 10, 2008, from http://gallery.carnegiefoundation.org/ilyons

Lytle, S. (1997). *On reading teacher research: Focus on basics.* Retrieved November 18, 2008, from http://www.ncsall.net/?id=480

Ma, L. (1999). *Knowing and teaching elementary school mathematics.* Mahwah, NJ: Lawrence Erlbaum Associates.

MERLin, University of British Columbia. (1998). *Points of viewing children's thinking companion website.* Retrieved August 15, 2008, from http://www.pointsofviewing.org

MERLOT. (2008). *Multimedia educational resource for learning and online teaching.* Retrieved August 14, 2008, from http://www.merlot.org/merlot/index.htm

Metropolitan Life/Harris Interactive. (2003). *Metlife survey of the American teacher.* New York: Metropolitan Life.

Moore, R. (2003). *Culturally engaged instruction: Putting theory into practice.* Retrieved March 24, 2008, from http://gallery.carnegiefoundation.org/collections/quest/collections/sites/moore_renee/

Morrison, T. (1987). *Beloved.* New York: Alfred A. Knopf.

Myers, J. (2006). *Living the life of a reader and writer.* Retrieved November 18, 2008, from http://cms.carnegiefoundation.org/collections/quest/collections/sites/myers_jennifer/

National Board for Professional Teaching Standards. (2001). *Leading from the classroom: Highlights from the 2001 NBPTS National Board Certified Teacher Leadership Survey conducted by Yankclovtch Partners.* Arlington, VA: NHITS. Available at: www.nbpts.org/pdf/leading.pdf

National Board for Professional Teaching Standards. (2008a). *Digital Edge Learning Interchange: Igniting conversation, imagination, and improvement in education.* Retrieved March 11, 2008, from http://ali.apple.com/ali_sites/deli/

National Board for Professional Teaching Standards. (2008b). "*The Portfolio.*" Retrieved February 4, 2008, from http://www.nbpts.org/for_candidates/the_portfolio

National Center for Restructuring Education, Schools, and Teaching. (2008). *About us: History.* Retrieved August 15, 2008, from http://www.tc.edu/ncrest/history.htm

Noyce Foundation. (2007a). *Inside Writing Workshop.* Retrieved January 15, 2008, from http://www.InsideWritingWorkshop.org

Noyce Foundation. (2007b). *Inside Writing Workshop: Professional study within learning communities.* Retrieved March 24, 2008, from http://www.insidewritingworkshop.org/profdev/

Noyce Foundation. (2008a). *Every child a reader and writer: Literacy coaching in support of writers workshop.* Retrieved March 24, 2008, from http://www.noycefdn.org/literacy/documents/LiteracyCoachinginSupportofWritersWorkshop07-08.pdf

Noyce Foundation. (2008b). *Every child a reader and writer: Outcomes for ECRW Schools.* Retrieved March 24, 2008, from http://www.noycefdn.org/literacy/documents/Outcomes07-08.pdf

Noyce Foundation. (2008c). *Living the Life of a Writer Studies*. Retrieved March 24, 2008, from http://www.noycefdn.org/literacy/lwl.html

Oakes, J., & Rogers, J. (2006). *Learning power: Organizing for education and justice*. New York: Teachers College Press.

Open Knowledge Initiatives. (2008). *Open Knowledge Initiative: Accelerated interoperability through simplified integration*. Retrieved August 15, 2008, from http://www.okiproject.org/view/html/node/382

Packer, S. (2008). *Welcome to Mrs. Packer's kindergarten website!* Retrieved March 11, 2008, from http://www.mrspacker.com/

Partridge, E., & Grossnickle Hines, A. (2003). *Whistling*. San Francisco: HarperCollins.

Pease-Alvarez, L. (2006). *Negotiating pedagogy in context*. Retrieved March 7, 2008, from http://www.cfkeep.org/html/stitch.php?s=69609704026589&id=930 29790365165

Pfitzner, A. (2003). *Looking beyond themselves: Preparing students to become invested members of their community*. Retrieved March 10, 2008, from http://gallery .carnegiefoundation.org/apfitzner

Pincus, M. (2001). *Playing with the possible: Teaching, learning, and drama on the second stage*. Retrieved March 10, 2008, from http://goingpublicwithteaching .org/mpincus/

Pincus, M. (2005). *Double double, toil and trouble: Engaging high school students in the study of Shakespeare*. Retrieved March 10, 2008, from http://quest.carnegie foundation.org/~dpointer/marshapincus/

Pointer, D. (2001). *Constructing bilingualism: Weaving a tapestry of language and culture in an English-instruction classroom*. Unpublished doctoral dissertation, University of California, Berkeley.

Pointer Mace, D. (2008). *Open the door!* Paper presented at the annual meeting of the American Association of Colleges of Teacher Education, New Orleans, LA.

Public Knowledge Project. (2008). *What is the public knowledge project?* Retrieved August 14, 2008, from http://pkp.sfu.ca/about

Rampersad, A. (2002). *The life of Langston Hughes: Volume I, 1902–1941, I, Too, Sing America*. Oxford: Oxford University Press.

Redmond, P. (2004). *The Teaching and Learning Interchange*. Retrieved August 15, 2008, from http://www.teachinginterchange.org/

Renz, H. (2008). *Welcome to Mrs. Renz's 4th grade class web site!* Retrieved March 11, 2008, from http://www2.redmond.k12.or.us/mccall/renz/

Richert, A. (2006). *Learning about adolescents from teachers who teach them well*. Retrieved February 24, 2008, from http://quest.carnegiefoundation.org/ ~arichert/

Robbins, J. (2002). *Creating parental permission and media release forms: 10 tips before posting student work online*. Retrieved March 11, 2008, from http://www .technologyintegrators.org/mediareleasesuggest.htm

Rose, M. (1995). *Possible lives: The promise of public education in America*. New York: Houghton Mifflin.

Ruff, W. (1991). *A call to assembly: The autobiography of a musical storyteller*. New York: Viking.

Rust, F., & Clark, C. (2007). *How to do action research in your classroom: Lessons from the teachers network leadership institute.* Retrieved August 18, 2008, from http://www.teachersnetwork.org/tnli/Action_Research_Booklet.pdf

Sawyers, L., Fountas, I., Pinnell, G. S., Scharer, P., & Walker, L. (2007). *Transforming teacher learning through design activity: Creating a web-based professional development support system for video case-based professional learning.* Paper presented at the annual meeting of the American Educational Research Association, Chicago.

Schomburg Center for Research in Black Culture. (2001). Harlem, 1900–1940: An *African-American community.* New York Public Library. Retrieved March 24, 2008, from http://www.si.umich.edu/CHICO/Harlem/index.html

Schultz, K. (2006). *Teaching and learning rituals and routines for literacy in elementary classrooms.* Retrieved March 7, 2008, from http://www.cfkeep.org/html/stitch.php?s=19117644819541&id=24383634351551

Schwab, J. J. (1973). The practical 3: Translation into curriculum. *School Review, 81,* 501–522.

Shulman, L. S. (2004). *The wisdom of practice: Essays on teaching, learning, and learning to teach.* San Francisco: Jossey Bass.

Shulman, L. (2005, September 1). To dignify the profession of the teacher: The Carnegie Foundation celebrates 100 years. *Change Magazine, 37*(9), 22.

Shulman, J., & Sato, M., Eds. (2006). *Mentoring teachers toward excellence: Supporting and developing highly qualified teachers.* San Francisco: Jossey-Bass.

Shulman, J., & Sharkey, E. (2006). Teaching note. In *Challenging student identity: Integrating Jewish studies into the history classroom.* Retrieved March 11, 2008, from http://www.cfkeep.org/html/stitch.php?s=94630557852453&id=17182043769566

SMMUSD. (2006). *School Accountability Report Card 2005–2006.* Retrieved March 25, 2008, from http://www.rogers.smmusd.org/pdf/SARCRogers.pdf

SMMUSD. (2008). *Will Rogers Learning Community School Accountability Report Card.* Retrieved August 15, 2008, from http://www.smmusd.org/sarc/SARC2007/RogersFinal0607ARC.pdf

State of California. (2008). *E-1 population estimates for cities, counties and the state with annual percent change—January 1, 2007 and 2008.* Retrieved August 16, 2008, from http://www.dof.ca.gov/research/demographic/reports/estimates/e-1_2006–07/documents/E-1table.xls

TeacherTube. (2008). *TeacherTube: Teach the world.* Retrieved August 15, 2008, from http://www.teachertube.com

Teachscape. (2008). *Teachscape: Reinventing professional learning.* Retrieved August 14, 2008, from http://teachscape.com/html/ts/nps/index.html

University of Michigan. (2008). *Knowledge networks on the web: Curriculum support for teaching, when you need it.* Retrieved August 15, 2008 from http://know.umich.edu/

Vander Wal, T. (2007). *Folksonomy coinage and definition.* Retrieved March 12, 2008, from http://vanderwal.net/folksonomy.html

Viadero, D. (2005). Scholars eye "signature" method of teacher training. *Education Week.* Retrieved November 18, 2008, from http://www.edweek.org/ew/articles/2005/10/12/07carnegie.h25.html

Wallace, B. (2006a). *The Noyce Foundation Every Child a Reader and Writer Unit Design: Process for planning a personal narrative unit.* Retrieved March 24, 2008, from http://www.insidewritingworkshop.org/profdev/materials/bw_unit process.pdf

Wallace, B. (2006b). *The Noyce Foundation Every Child a Reader and Writer Unit Design agenda.* Retrieved March 24, 2008, from http://www.insidewritingwork shop.org/profdev/materials/bw_agenda.pdf

Wikimedia Foundation. (2008). *Wikipedia: The free encyclopedia.* Retrieved August 15, 2008, from http://www.wikipedia.org

Wolk, E. (2002). *Pio Pico student researchers participatory action research: From classroom to community, transforming teaching and learning.* Retrieved March 10, 2008, from http://goingpublicwithteaching.org/ewolk/

Woodlands School. (2008). *Woodlands School: Vision. Woodlands School will become a national model and leader in the field of education.* Retrieved March 10, 2008, from http://woodlands-school.org/

Yahoo. (2008). *Flickr: Share your photos, watch the world.* Retrieved August 15, 2008, from http://www.flickr.com

Index

About the Author

D ÉSIRÉE POINTER MACE is an assistant professor of education at Alverno
College. Her work focuses on envisioning and inventing ways of representing teaching and learning using new media and online technologies. She has developed multimedia websites of exemplary practitioner
inquiry for many years, beginning with her work at the Carnegie Foundation for the Advancement of Teaching. There, Pointer Mace and Ann
Lieberman codirected the Goldman-Carnegie Quest Project for Signature
Pedagogies in Teacher Education, focused on the use of such websites in
preservice teacher education, and the Noyce-Carnegie Quest Project for
Elementary Literacy, which documented the relationship between classroom practice and professional development in elementary writing workshop. Pointer Mace and Lieberman are the founding coeditors of Inside
Teaching, a "living archive" of teaching practice.

Pointer Mace taught elementary school for many years as a Spanish
bilingual teacher and bilingual resource specialist in the Oakland and
San Francisco Unified School Districts. She has worked with students from
kindergarten through doctoral level in the United States, the Dominican
Republic, and Ecuador. She holds a BA in cognitive science from Vassar
College and an MA and PhD in education with a concentration in
language, literacy, and culture from UC Berkeley. She lives in Milwaukee,
Wisconsin, with her husband, Michael Pointer Mace, and her children,
Simone and Myles.